Don't Shoot!

I'm a Detached Youth Worker

Mike Burgess and Inez Burgess

Russell House Publishing

First published in 2006 by:
Russell House Publishing Ltd.
4 St. George's House
Uplyme Road
Lyme Regis
Dorset DT7 3LS

Tel: 01297-443948
Fax: 01297-442722
e-mail: help@russellhouse.co.uk
www.russellhouse.co.uk

Dedicated to Luke, Zoe and Ella – our children, who wonder why we've spent so long on the computer writing!

British Library Cataloguing-in-publication Data:
A catalogue record for this book is available from the British Library.

ISBN: 1-903855-95-0
       978-1-903855-95-9

Design and layout by Jeremy Spencer
Printed by Cromwell Press, Trowbridge

About Russell House Publishing

RHP is a group of social work, probation, education and youth and community work practitioners and academics working in collaboration with a professional publishing team.

Our aim is to work closely with the field to produce innovative and valuable materials to help managers, trainers, practitioners and students.

We are keen to receive feedback on publications and new ideas for future projects.

For details of our other publications please visit our website or ask us for a catalogue. Contact details are on this page.

Contents

About the Authors iv

Acknowledgements iv

Introduction 1

Chapter 1 Don't Shoot! I'm a Detached Youth Worker 5
Starting Out: Reconnaissance Period

Chapter 2 Let's Talk About Feelings: A Risky Business 15
Detached Youth Work with Young Men: Practical Guidelines

Chapter 3 Look Before You Leap 25
Detached Youth Work with Young Women: A Male Approach

Chapter 4 Are You up for it? 27
Relationship Building with Individuals and Groups

Chapter 5 Welcome to Las Vegas, North-East Style 41
Issue Based Work: Gambling

Chapter 6 Every Individual Has the Right to 30% Unemployment! 49
Issue Based Work: Employment

Chapter 7 Cowboys or Indians? 57
Work with Other Agencies and Partnerships

Chapter 8 Leading the Troops out of the Trenches 61
Managing Detached Youth Work

Chapter 9 Flying by the Seat of my Pants: A Celebration 65
Celebrating Detached Youth Work

References 69

Appendices 70

Appendix 1 Sample Job Description 70

Appendix 2 Sample Detached Youth Work Guidelines 74

Appendix 3 Induction Pack 82

Appendix 4 Probationary Non-managerial Agreement 85

Appendix 5 Federation for Detached Youth Work 86

Appendix 6 Sample Recording and Evaluation Form 87

Appendix 7 Sample Recording and Evaluation Sheet for an Interagency Visit 88

Appendix 8 Risk Assessment Policy 89

Appendix 9 Employment Strategy 91

Appendix 10 The Longbenton Ladder to Success 92

About the Authors

Mike Burgess has been a detached youth worker in the North-East since 1989 and presently is the project manager for the Phoenix Detached Youth Work Project in the Meadow Well, North Shields.

Inez Burgess is a primary teacher in Durham.

Following a challenging educational experience at secondary school it is a rewarding experience to now be an informal educator. We hope to motivate others into entering a valuable and effective aspect of the profession.

Unravelling the jottings and ramblings of Mike's professional thoughts was indeed a complex and entertaining task! We have spent many a long evening writing a book which we hope will be of use to all those wanting to enter or already working in detached youth work.

Acknowledgements

Gordon Brown – for creating effective cartoons for the book.

Tony James – for transferring remarkably accurate observations into cartoons for Mike when he left Longbenton Youth Project and allowing the use of them within the book.

Tim Burke – for promoting detached youth work via various articles, covering work in all the projects I've been involved with, in *Young People Now*. Also, for allowing these to be used in the book.

Andy Goudling – for working jointly with Mike and producing the guidelines for detached youth work with men.

Bill Cox and the Liverpool Youth Service – for allowing the use of their detached youth work guidelines.

David McGuigan and Becky Rowe – for being supportive colleagues and co-workers at Longbenton Youth Project, as is Kerry Douglas, who presently works with Mike at the Phoenix Detached Youth Project.

Steve Barrigan – for being my mentor and non-managerial supervisor since 1989.

Keith Tate – for his construction front cover for LYP's construction report.

To the many workers, students, part-timers and workers from other agencies, who have been influential in the success of Mike's work as discussed in the book.

Last, but not least, to all the young people who make the job worthwhile, for without them this book would not have been written.

Introduction

Following many years of listening to her partner Mike about his experiences as a detached youth worker, Inez Burgess suggested that it would be valuable to share what he had learnt with others. Although there are several good books on detached work written by academics and researchers, very little has been written by those who actually do the job. They therefore decided to produce this practical guide in the hope that it would support and inspire both experienced and new workers, and others employed in the human services, to value and use detached youth work as a means of social and personal education as well as a means of helping and supporting socially disadvantaged young people.

About detached youth work

Detached youth work happens when workers go out onto the streets, or other places where young people meet, to form relationships with those for whom more traditional styles of youth work either don't exist, or where commercial youth provision is unaffordable, inappropriate or fails to meet their needs. The relationship between the detached youth worker and the young person is built on the mutual trust and respect that develops, on the young person's terms. The workers are then better able to identify a young person's needs because they will be more inclined to share information about their lives with someone they have a trusting relationship with. Detached work also allows the worker to employ a person-centred, holistic approach to the work, gaining a unique insight into the areas of concern for the young people they meet because the focus of the work is the whole person and their developmental needs, not a particular problem or difficulty. Once these needs are identified, the workers can give information, provide practical assistance, offer emotional support during times of stress, and undertake counselling to help youngsters through key transitions in their lives. But there is an equally important role to be played in helping youngsters get the most out of being young, by assisting them to organise activities and projects and facilitating trips, residential weekends away and holidays.

Detached youth work is a valuable method of working with young people in a wide variety of social settings because of its adaptability, flexibility and responsiveness. Detached workers will often identify and support young people in crisis, and this will mean them working outside the 9-5 working hours of most other agencies and organisations. It can provide focused support for young people within the communities in which they live, and on the street corners where they congregate.

Many detached work projects are based in areas of social disadvantage and high unemployment, where young people face a multitude of disadvantages and often feel socially excluded. Therefore, a detached youth worker working in such an area will face a diverse and challenging range of issues affecting young people's lives. Many of these issues, unemployment, mental health, addiction and masculinity are discussed in this book.

About this book

We have written this book as a practical guide to show how the theory of detached work can be linked to the practice. We hope that it will enable youth workers and managers to develop effective methods of working with young people; enabling them to explore life choices and encouraging positive change, personally and socially, as members of their community. This book highlights the fun and enjoyment, challenges and difficulties, involved in the process of delivering detached youth work, through the experiences of Mike Burgess.

Who will benefit from this book?

This book is written with a lot of different readers in mind:

- **Students** of youth work, social work and Connexions, will find new, and probably quite surprising, approaches to the day-to-day problems they will face.

- **New detached youth workers** will, hopefully, pick up some 'tricks of the trade' but also gain some new perspectives on the work and what it is possible to achieve with a little ingenuity and a sense of humour. As David Crimmens and his colleagues found in their recent study of detached youth work (Crimmens *et al.*, 2004), this is an expanding field and new workers with backgrounds in health, careers, community safety and urban renewal won't necessarily have the same grounding in detached work as youth workers. Hopefully, this book could save them from having to 're-invent the wheel' too often.

- **Experienced detached workers** may want to use this book to compare notes. In detached work we learn a lot from one another's experience and, in this case, we've simply written that experience down.

- **Other youth workers** may find that some of the approaches outlined in this book could complement their existing approaches and extend their repertoire.

- **Project managers and committee members** may find that managing detached youth work isn't always easy, not least because these days most funders want quick results and 'results' in detached work sometimes take a little time. Hopefully this book will boost their confidence in the method and enable them to offer their workers support through the early days, when the hard, and often unrewarding, grind of making contact has to be done.

- **Funders** should read this book. They need to understand what they are investing in and why they must be realistic in terms of timescales. But they also need to know what an excellent investment detached work is.

- **Professionals in other agencies** need to read this book because, in an era of multi-agency working, they cannot afford to ignore the invaluable contribution of detached work in the fields of child welfare, sexual health, mental health, employment, education and training and community safety and youth offending.

- **Elected members**, for much the same reason, need to read this book so that the decisions they make about funding and the development of services for children and young people are 'evidence-based'.

Detached Youth Work: A Brief Bibliography

Crimmens, D., Factor, F., Jeffs, T., Pitts, J., Pugh, C., Spence, J. and Turner, P. (2004) *Reaching Socially Excluded Young People: A National Study of Street-based Youth Work*. Leicester: Joseph Rowntree Foundation/NYA.

This book is based on a national study of detached youth work undertaken between 2001 and 2003. It offers a picture of the nature, scale and distribution of detached work in England and Wales and studies 11 projects in depth. It points to the changing nature of detached work and its role in multi-agency interventions with young people at risk, in need and in trouble.

France, A. and Wiles, P. (1996) *The Youth Action Scheme*. London: DfEE.

This report gives an account of a DfEE-funded experimental project that used detached work method to target young people at risk of, or involved in, crime. The project was deemed to be a modest success but it highlights many of the tensions and dilemmas that can arise from undertaking narrowly targeted work.

Goetschius, G. and Tash, J. (1967) *Working with Unattached Youth: Problem, Approach and Method*. London: Routledge.

This classic action research study is based on a project organised around a tea stall in central London. In many ways it laid down the blueprint for modern detached youth work. The book explains the 'whys' and 'hows' of detached work in considerable detail and still has a great deal of relevance today.

Harris, P. (2005) Curriculum Debate and Detached Work. *Youth and Policy*. No.87, Spring.

This article continues the discussion about the relevance of a 'youth work curriculum' by looking at how the idea of a curriculum can be pursued in a detached youth work setting.

Johnson, L., MacDonald, R., Mason, P., Ridley, L. and Webster, C. *Snakes and Ladders: Young People, Transitions and Social Exclusion*. York: Joseph Rowntree Foundation.
   This report, based on research on a low-income, high-crime, housing estate, details the kinds of problems faced by young people in areas of high unemployment. Many were out of school and few were in touch with any welfare or educational agency. The report concludes that only detached youth work is likely to be effective in making contact with them.

Kaufman, S. (2001) 'Detached Youth Work'. In Factor, F., Chauhan, V. and Pitts, J. *The RHP Companion to Working with Young People*. Lyme Regis: Russell House Publishing.
   This chapter gives a brief history of the origins and development of detached work in the UK and outlines the detached work process.

Chapter 1

Don't Shoot! I'm a Detached Youth Worker

Starting Out: Reconnaissance Period

Starting out in town

Detached youth workers, whether new or established, must always ensure that making and maintaining contact on the streets remains the foundation for effective work. However, whether you are a new worker in an established project or an experienced worker beginning a new project, it is essential that a reconnaissance period takes place. This could take place between three to eight months and will allow the workers to gain an overall understanding of the area. Reconnaissance needs to include preparation, walking the streets, contact making, meeting agencies, conclusions and recommendations for the future development of the project and how it fits into the local community.

My experiences:

Interview preparation: Detached youth workers don't write!

Interview: The first fly by the seat of my pants!

First day at work: PANIC!

Job description: What a fantastic job! I get paid for walking around and talking to people. (If I can understand them – Geordie/Sand-dancer's lingo is not quite the same as Manchester slang!) **But** a detached worker's greeting, apart from the dreaded silence, is similar in all languages: 'Who the F*** are **you**!'

Dress code: Should I die my hair? Roll a fag? Wear a badge? I bought some red shoes as I had very little hair!

Arrival at premises: The second fly by the seat of my pants: literally, slipping on a fish-head into our offices – the sea angling hut, on the pier, next to the fairground in South Shields. Fish-heads were a regular Monday morning greeting, winking at me from the bin.

Reconnaissance: Who can spell it, never mind know how to do it? Hopefully you'll be more prepared! Here's my approach, it may help.

MIKE & DAVE in the COMMUNITY!?

HEY LADS, I know graffiti provides you kids with an outlet to express yourselves artistically and personally, but many members of the community, particularly the elderly, find it offensive and intimidating. If you come to LYP we can help you redirect your anger and challenge your behaviour...

See Dave, if you treat them with respect, they'll treat you with RESPECT!!!

My approach to reconnaissance

This may differ slightly depending upon the patch you will be working in or whether your project is new or established. The following will provide a good starting point.

Preparation

- Set up the office base (a good way to get to know your co-worker).

- Read and understand your job description and check its relevancy (example Appendix 1).

- Read detached work guidelines, if available (example Appendix 2).

- In an established project there should be an induction pack that should be completed with your line manager. For new projects an induction pack needs to be designed so it is relevant to detached youth work (example Appendix 3).

- Discuss areas of need and concerns with the management.

- Identify a non-managerial supervisor who is independent from your organisational structure. (Preferably an experienced detached youth worker, still working in the field. Ask other workers for suggestions. See Appendix 4 for an example of Probationary Non-managerial Agreement for Year 1). This is a vital professional support mechanism that should be paid for by your employer in work's time. If there is no provision for this you must argue that this is your first training need.

- Contact the Federation for Detached Youth Work to identify your Regional Detached Youth Workers Forum, for support, to share ideas and if needed to find a non-managerial supervisor (see Appendix 5 for details of the Federation).

- Establish recording and evaluating system for visits to agencies and detached youth work (both need to be designed to give specific information (for examples see Appendices 6 and 7).

- Identify administrative support.

> In my first project I asked my line manager for administrative support and was presented with a type-writer. My thoughts were – not much use to a one finger specialist! Time to use my detached work skills – had a walk round the town hall, saw a door marked Educational Typists, sauntered in, gave them some patter, job's a good one! Cost – plenty of funny tales, laughter and a box of chocolates for the Annual Report. Remember utilise your skills well!

- Design and make ID cards with photographs, signed by employers or get official ID from the local authority.

- Identify a solicitor to contact if arrested by the police.

- Arrange building and liability insurance.

- Design a contact card and leaflet explaining the background to the project, what is detached youth work and your approach to the work.

- With the cards and leaflets visit agencies and community groups. Identify those who could work well with young people and those who could help improve the service delivery.

- Detached youth work should not be a cheap option. A well planned project will allow for an annual clothing allowance, usually for coat and shoes.

- Street work expenses can be very important in certain patches and need to be formalised and supported by the management. Have an awareness that sometimes receipts are difficult to obtain, due to 'street cred'.

Walkabout

Identify the patch that you are able to walk to from the base. Make this your geographical area (not too big). Detached youth work is not crime prevention led or specific to certain hotspots, but should be inclusive of all young people within your geographical area.

Detached youth work is often confused with outreach work. Both are effective methods of working but differ in their aims and objectives.

Outreach work is the extension of work linked to a base. It is a style of work where workers go out from a youth centre/youth offending team/drugs project/crime prevention for the police, for example, to promote an issue and encourage them to return to using a building. This style of working can also be very effective but only for those young people willing to remain within the setting of the building.

As stated by the Federation for Detached Youth Work the core values in detached youth work are:

- The relationship with the young people remains voluntary.

- The service we deliver is 'needs led'.

- The power base remains with young people and not the workers.

Making and maintaining contact on the streets is the backbone of detached youth work. I believe it is the key to effective detached work for new and established projects. Detached workers contact and work with young people on their own terms, on their own territory, be it a street corner, an amusement arcade or a coffee bar. Without a building, pool table or table tennis to lend security, a detached worker is exposed and relies heavily on inter-personal skills. A building can impose constraints that affect the role of the youth worker and can inhibit the responses of young people who may identify themselves as being in opposition to authority figures.

When Mike Burgess, the Longbenton Legend, annoyingly disturbed Jonny Wilkinson's kicking practice on the eve of the Rugby Union World Cup final to ask him the quickest way to Meadowell, angry Jonny willingly obliged, immediately pointing him in the right direction, and in doing so, gave a whole new meaning to the descriptive term of 'detached' youth worker!!!

Because detached work happens on the streets, rather than in a building, it is often seen as an unstructured or 'maverick' style of work by other youth workers and young people alike.

In practice, the opposite tends to be the case; the work needs to be clearly structured if any progress or development is to be made. We use weekly recordings to review and plan the street work and group work we do.

Our street work helps us to identify groups of young people to approach and work with in more depth. Once contact has been established, mutual respect and relationships can be developed at the young person's own pace. As workers, we are very much a guest in the young person's environment, so we have to use our youth work skills in our own individual adapted style. The direction of our group work and project work is developed with young people: our recordings help us to monitor and evaluate that work.

Burgess, 1991.

Initial work in areas should always take place in pairs, for safety and accusation issues. Discuss with your co-worker how your different personalities and style will affect your working practice.

Walk the streets to become knowledgeable of routes, names, amenities, community facilities and identify places young people congregate etc. During initial walkabouts avoid contact with young people, for safety and initial observations, both for you and the young people.

On returning from walkabout record and evaluate detached youth work sessions. Discuss the findings and the patch.

Identify groups of young people in patch and record any relevant dialogue linked to issues and needs, e.g. racism, equal opportunities, interests, young people's ideas to develop. Remember to assess any risks in location, access and safety.

It is required by insurance companies to have a risk assessment policy for detached youth workers (see Appendix 8).

Making contact or 'The Maverick Approach to Youth Work'

A good starting point is to visit the agencies that work with young people on the estate or patch. You will be able to discuss the issues relevant to the local area and explore their involvement and service they deliver to the young people. This will enable you to assess the future links and joint work that could be possible. Developing work with other agencies is discussed in Chapter 7.

Before talking with young people discuss with your co-worker which group to approach first, (usually a group which appear to be approachable) who's going to speak and what you will say. Discuss your individual styles of communicating with young people. Try to complement and develop a way of working as a team using your individual strengths. Be aware of when your colleague is struggling so you can interact. Remember different styles will suit different groups of young people, but your priority is to create a fun and positive experience as a guest in the young people's environment.

Consider how well you know the group you have chosen to approach and your potential exit routes and safety. Certain areas where young people hang out, e.g. in a dark dead-end alley, need 'on the spot' risk assessment. Agree a signal for departure as it may be needed. For example, be aware of your co-worker whilst talking with a group as you may need to consider types of conflict or body language that may be displayed by the young people.

For safety, stand at least an arm's length away from a young person as this gives you space to manoeuvre if a young person becomes aggressive. Also if you stand side on to a young person who could become aggressive, it is more difficult for them to hit you. Making a young person laugh is a good method to diffuse aggression. Be aware not to be encircled.

When you are feeling positive and in a good frame of mind you can attempt contact. Assess by observation which group could be most approachable for first contact. This gives you an opportunity to build up slowly towards contacting more difficult groups and allows you to gain more confidence and develop your skills. Even negative experiences of contacting young people, for example, your introduction is met by silence, are all part of the learning process.

In the early stages the value of analysing the group dynamics and type of dialogue with young people, needs to be discussed and recorded at the end of the session on evaluation sheets.

Often on early contact making the mistake is to offer activities and trips straight away. This can lead to conflict as you are trying to move at your pace rather than the young person's. If you go ahead with taking them on a trip you are removing them from an unstructured environment on their terms to a structured environment where boundaries are needed. Just as you would not go on holiday with a new friend you have met in the pub, the same applies to new contacts, as they are unknown quantities.

However, there is a fine line between talking too long on the street corner without action and acting too quickly. Experience and the type of group will eventually determine the type and speed of progress.

Following successful contact, time needs to be spent on the streets with the young people. This will continually take place by an effective detached youth work project whether one or ten years old.

Listening carefully to young people's thoughts allows a good detached youth worker to develop a whole range of dialogue, as well as gaining information about the basic picture of young people's needs. It is stated in the Joseph Rowntree report into streetwork, '…dialogue, and a willingness to begin with the issues and questions that have significance for the young person, may well be a pre-requisite for success…' (Crimmens *et al.*, 2004). When this is carried out effectively the big issues affecting the young people in your patch are easily identified, for example in South Shields young people were specifically affected by gambling in the arcades.

After a 5-8 month period a reconnaissance report should be written. It should include the following:

- A mission statement.

- Clear indications of how detached youth work will link with the community.

- Name which agencies are useful to work in partnerships with.

- Ongoing objectives for the day-to-day running of the project.

- Developmental aims and objectives which will change each year depending upon the relevant issues affecting the young people on the estate/patch at that time.

After 16 years of face to face detached youth work the challenging and amusing experiences on the street still motivate me and give me great pleasure.

One incident I still re-tell was that of when I was in South Shields on a cold, wet night. Turning the corner into the local park I was intrigued to hear yelping and laughter. As the bowling green came into sight a big lad, who was known to me, was hooting with laughter as he was joyfully shooting people in their backsides with an air gun. I was only saved when he raised the gun on me by quickly shouting, 'Don't shoot me, I'm a detached youth worker!' Luckily he started laughing and at this point I shot off into the distance as quickly as possible, with my co-worker running even faster than me!

So, remember you'll never be bored or sure what surprise the night's going to bring when you set off to walk the streets!

Don't shoot me, I'm a detached youth worker!

Chapter 2

Let's Talk About Feelings: A Risky Business

Detached Youth Work with Young Men: Practical Guidelines

As professional workers detached work with young men is only one piece of a complex workload. It can be a challenging but effective method in assisting young men in their personal and social educational development. Many young men often find their roles within society can be contradictory. They are expected to be tough and macho with their peers, whilst being sensitive to others within their relationships. They are within the transition from youth to adulthood and often have no-one or no place to discuss their feelings. Many young men are often mentally in crisis and feel isolated, which then can develop into macho behaviour, violence, failure in education and depression. Therefore, it is essential that an environment is created where young men can explore their masculinity and the contradiction of being young and male.

It is important to highlight that it can be equally valuable for both male and female workers to develop good practice in this area of detached work. Through many years of experience I have found that good practice can only be achieved through a combination of developing theory and then, effectively linking this to practice. One without the other provides a service of little value for young men. The following guidelines enable workers to enhance their theoretical understanding of working with young men by providing them with a practical, progressively staged approach.

The progressive areas of development are:

1. Individual exploration of self, theory and training in work with young men.

2. Contacting men and developing positive dialogue in their own environment.

3. The holistic approach to working with men in a detached work setting and beyond.

1. Individual exploration of self, theory and training in work with young men

Exploration of self – in head

The remainder of this chapter contains a number of bullets points and guidelines which were produced for the Detached Youth Workers Conference by Mike Burgess and Andy Goulding (Burgess and Goulding, 1999).

• **Be prepared to talk about your own masculinity and feelings and be honest. You can't expect young men to take the risks if you won't.**

It is necessary for individual exploration of self to occur prior to contact with young men. It should be undertaken in both professional and informal environments.

Exploration for men

Many male detached workers have to face an uncomfortable dilemma here because individual exploration of your own masculinity, maleness, learnt sexism and feelings, need to be explored, for often the first time in your own lifetime! It is vital that male workers create time and space to talk about being a young man growing up, relationships with their own father or son, learnt sexism and their own feelings.

I found that attending courses or training on the theory of work with young men was an informative beginning. Also talking to other men in this environment provided me with positive motivation needed to explore my own self further. Additional ways to further this exploration are to try role-play and to create dialogue with the help of practical resources, e.g. board games, challenging posters. All of these activities develop confidence and your understanding of self, and you are then ready to take a risk in working with men in a detached work setting.

Exploration for women

Many women workers often have excellent skills in using discussion and dialogue around feelings and needs. However, it is also important that women attend training and discuss with male workers the theories behind masculinity, maleness and work with men. An awareness of the theories and statistics behind men's changing roles will assist women to have a balanced approach, linking positive work to challenging sexist behaviour.

It is important to remember that it is the young men who will make the decision of who they work with or talk to – male or female workers. Female and male workers can develop different, equally valuable, approaches to working with men in a detached work setting and beyond. All you have to do is to be prepared and take the risk.

2. Contacting men and developing positive dialogue in their own environment

- **Be aware you are a guest in the young people's environment if you challenge sexist behaviour. Remember that males in an all male environment or mixed group often increase their sexist behaviour.**

Prepared with theoretical knowledge and self awareness, the difficult task of linking theory to practice can now begin. Your initial contact and responses as youth workers to young men's behaviour could decide if and when future relationships with them can develop.

It is again necessary to be prepared by discussing with colleagues how you will operate in a detached work setting. Areas of discussion should include early identification of professional responses to sexist behaviour or other comments such as racism, aggressive behaviour etc. This is not such an easy task as it is vital to remember you are a guest in the young people's environment and also at risk.

Whilst undergoing reconnaissance period at a newly established project on a large housing estate, myself and my colleague experienced similar difficulties as described above. Initial contact with large groups often resulted in the group displaying macho, aggressive non-verbal responses to our presence. Alongside the absence of dialogue there was an increase in negative behaviour towards other residents. They enjoyed the responses given by the residents, thus reinforcing society's view of a group of young men being a powerful threat to the residents of the community.

Men are often under massive pressure from their peers to be macho, sex symbols, risk takers and fearless. Individually they can be vulnerable but this is often hidden by aggression and threatening actions in their group. It should then be apparent that initial contact making is not the wise time to challenge negative behaviour. It is important to develop relationships, partake in positive work and build relationships. It is only over a substantial period of time that you will be able to successfully question challenging behaviour and have the young person respond positively, or question their own values and actions.

- **Be aware of your personal safety, get to know the group and develop a positive relationship.**

To challenge young men's sexist, aggressive or negative behaviour towards others before you have developed an effective dialogue or shared experiences, such as an activity, can put your personal safety at risk. Relationships develop with young men at their pace and on their terms. They will judge you by what you say, or more importantly, by your practical actions towards them. It is therefore important to evaluate each detached session both orally with other workers and in a written format for your records. It will enable you to monitor a group's progress and help you to assess the development of individual relationships.

- **Try to talk about what is positive about being male; some interesting dialogue can happen. Try to find some commonalities e.g. positive relationships with older males, (fathers, brothers).**

Try to create dialogue about what is positive about being male. Keep it lively, interesting and fun. Also remember different approaches work for different people and in different situations. Listen carefully to conversation. Often a comment about a dad or son allows the worker to slip in a leading question about the young man's positive male experiences.

Occasionally take a risk and talk about some of the positive aspects of being male.

I did this about becoming a dad for the first time. One young man, who was the leader of his group, was in the same situation at sixteen. I commented that it was an amazing feeling being a dad and seeing a baby which had your features for the first time. His initial response after experiencing the same emotional experience, was to launch into a five minute surge of feelings about his experiences. Following this he realised that his mates did not know how to respond to his experience and he then made negative responses about his girlfriend, to cover up his embarrassment. Even though the young man had broken an unspoken rule not to talk about his feelings in his group, he had also started a personal development in our relationship, as a youth worker and client.

Following dialogue, further exploration of how men in the group think, will be useful to you to assess the developmental route for that group and the individuals in it.

A method that has worked with my groups is to make a list of what is positive and negative about being male. You will find the positive list will be a lot shorter and more difficult to write than the negative list. How do you respond? Look at the list of positive statements and devise a range of open ended questions to create positive dialogue about being male.

For example
Men don't have to shave their legs or give birth to children, are often seen as good positive answers received from groups of young men. This can lead to discussion about men's involvement in birth, and relevant male behaviour and responsibility of male parents.

Following the exploration of the positives of being male a holistic approach to men's range of complex needs is the third and final progression in working with young men.

3. The holistic approach to working with men in a detached work setting and beyond

There are various important issues to understand whilst developing the holistic approach with young men, both in groups and individually. Flexibility in your approach must take priority when on the street.

- **Once you have established contacts try to target young men who have group influence. Build up relationships with them outside their peer group.**

This can be undertaken in a detached work setting in their own environment. It is vital to use the following guidelines whilst working with the young men:

- **Have an awareness that young men are in crisis. It is important we become aware of their needs as men, not negative images that society gives them.**
- **Work with the young men holistically on issues that they feel they fail or fear, for example, employment, health, education, relationships, sexuality.**
- **It is important to ask if they are OK.**

Remember, you can't deal with only one aspect of a person's life. Be aware of the complete person, particularly mental health. It is a well known fact that the second biggest killer of young men is suicide.

Feelings, mental health, men don't talk

Following the exploration of the positives of being male you can now develop work which involves the negative aspects of masculinity. Youth workers will now be able to challenge learnt sexism and negative behaviour of men towards others, women and men. This stage will though take a long time to reach.

- Often young men are in conflict with their masculinity and feelings. They often feel that to become more powerful and to gain stature amongst their peers they should target more vulnerable men and women for abuse. This must be challenged.

> One example of this is whilst a colleague and myself were on street work in an arcade a young lad, on the fringe of a group, whilst not using eye contact gave verbal abuse to us, hence displaying macho behaviour. Whilst leaving the lions den that night and over a period of time, it became apparent that the vocal young man was in fact regularly put down in front of his peers. After repeated violent incidents over the following year, we helped him overcome his submissiveness to the violence inflicted on him by cigarette burns, helping him value himself and others through one to one work. He eventually rebuilt his life and gained employment. This was an example of developing positive dialogue from a negative beginning.

Often young men, seen as negative by society, increase their negative behaviour to cover up the mental crisis, unable to discuss it with anyone. You, as youth workers, can then use the opportunity to develop awareness whilst challenging, appropriately, language and behaviour.

- There are limitations developing groupwork with young men on the streets. Use detached work sessions to encourage men to attend groups. This often can take months of asking.

- Create a secure space where men feel comfortable to talk about their feelings. It may be a risky business, but it is always very rewarding.

Use this practical guide to assist you in your work but remember:
Be prepared, be flexible and take a risk: the rewards for you and your clients are tangible.

Issue based work: young dads

Starting point
As a male on a youth and community work training course you can feel at fault for everything i.e. constant discussion about the way you oppress women. Then you're told by everyone to go off and work with young men…(**not** a good starting point)…

I know that as a man and a youth worker I felt uncomfortable about the work I was expected to do – I was confused and it wasn't working. Why should you expect men to sit down and dwell on what's negative. After attending a conference I realised that a good starting point was to look at ourselves as men and to do things that are positive and celebratory, for it is only then that progressive, lasting change can be made by analysing your treatment of women and other people.

When I arrived in Longbenton I discussed my interest in working with men to staff at the Barnardo's family centre on the estate. Later that year a group of men expressed the need for a support group at the centre.

In partnership with Adrian, a social worker, this led to a Young Men's Support Group with an initial aim of offering a forum for men aged 16 plus to discuss their feelings, particularly around fatherhood. In Longbenton male unemployment at that time was 70%. Few of the men on the estate could expect to bring in an income and with other issues such as poverty, violence, crime and drugs, it was a challenge raising children on the estate.

After a year the one positive area the group had in common was – being dads. This led to a project with Keith, an artist. The group took photographs of themselves doing positive tasks with their children. This then led to a photographic display of twelve photographs. The group then took part in discussions around the positives and negatives of being a dad.

Following this the group then decided to produce 'The Canny Dads' pack, which included posters and discussion cards. The pack was aimed at 16 year olds for schools and youth organisations, to create discussion around the issues of violence/ domestic violence and comparing this with positive images of dads. This was a hugely successful educational pack and was eventually sold worldwide, creating a substantial income for the project which benefited the dads.

Tim Burke of *Young People Now* joined a group work session with the young dads. His article following this session stated:

> An item on Radio 4 'Today' programme focused on how unemployed young men were often an economic liability on young mothers who lost benefit if there was a man around. Men were pushed towards a 'twilight world', flitting in and out of their families lives, living on the fringes of their society. No chance of a job, widely perceived only as a burden or a threat – it is not surprising they feel under pressure. Group member Billy summed it up as 'depressed, frustrated, inadequate – the feeling that I don't provide for my family'. They discovered a

huge need among young men to talk in a secure, trusting environment… We expected it to take several months before we got down to the nitty-gritty, but what actually happened was as soon as they had a space that was theirs – oomph! – there was a massive offload.

John, a member of the group, sees the group and contact with the youth workers as the means of his salvation. With a history of a broken family, unhappy time in care, problems with drugs and homelessness, and the breakdown of the relationship with the mother of his child, John carries a heavy burden. He is desperate to get his life sorted, and maintain and build a positive relationship with his son.

John continued, 'I watched the detached workers from a distance and when I was satisfied that they were alright I approached them…I hadn't anyone to turn to. But I needed to talk about things – get it off my chest. Mike has been on the blunt end of a lot from me but has been behind me all the way…there's a lot of confidence and trust built up. I can feel all the emotions pulling on me and just talking about it is a big relief. This group gives me space, they're comfortable listening to us gabbing off'.

'New Man, New Masculinity', *Young People Now*, Burke, 1996.

Eventually as the Canny Dads group became established I was able to encourage other young dads I met via detached youth work, to access the group successfully.

The value of working holistically with both parents needs to be considered. In my experience it is far better to develop work with the mum and dad, both jointly and in single gender groups. This allows the worker to objectively challenge negative behaviour, whilst supporting positive development. Again it needs to be stressed that detached youth work should use the bottom-up approach of working with young dads. An example of this is when the government realised the importance of working with teenage dads. We were well placed, due to our holistic approach and relationships with young dads, to do a poster project aimed at supporting young dads.

For young, teenage dads fatherhood can be a frightening prospect. Supporting and encouraging a teenage dads' group to develop new skills was a very positive experience for both dads and workers. The teenage dads' group was successfully involved in activities with their children leading to discussions about health promotion. This culminated in the production of a poster set of teenage dads for health clinics and doctors surgeries. The posters (see page 24) were aimed at making young men positively explore and question their role of being a dad, as well as realising the need for support.

Chapter 3

Look Before You Leap

Detached Youth Work with Young Women: A Male Approach

As a male worker it is important to deliver the best service possible to all young people in your patch. In my view a good professional detached youth worker should be able to, and strive to, work with both men and women, whether they are a male or female worker.

Whilst working in Longbenton the two professionals appointed were both male. As a long-term strategy our aim was to increase the staff team to include a female worker. However, initially we had to increase the use of the project to young women by stating, 'The project is for you as well as the lads. The lads are getting loads out of the project. You need to get involved to get your fair share of LYP's services'. After our first year, even though we were two male workers, around 50% of contacts with DYW were women.

In my opinion and my experience, young people will make their own choices about who they will trust and who they will not accept help from. Often men prefer to use the female worker and women choose to use the male worker. Clients will make their own choice.

Without stating the obvious, it is very important that when work is planned by a male worker with young women, it is vital to avoid leaving yourself or the young women vulnerable, leading to accusations of misconduct. From my experience it is good practice to encourage a group of at least two or three women to come into the office base together to plan a trip, rather than one on their own. The project should draft guidelines about areas for the male worker to consider when working with young women.

Good practice should be shared and discussed between workers, for example no touching for reassurance, and to be aware of over-familiar, flirtatious or tactile young people. Women who are nervous or uncomfortable in the presence of a male worker may prefer a female worker. It may appear obvious but by producing guidelines all parties involved will be protected, as well as being aware of good practice.

Professional discussion between workers around working with women helps to raise awareness of women's needs and issues, as well as support and develop a male worker's practice.

In the street work setting it is important that when creating dialogue with groups to remember that it is also an arena to promote equal opportunities. Different dynamics of equality can be observed within mixed groups. I worked with one mixed group, of young men and women of similar age, who exhibited dynamics that were driven by young women who were respected and powerful within the group. This group operated equally and worked more effectively as a group.

Alternatively another mixed group, consisting of younger women and older men, exhibited different dynamics. The men gave the women little respect, disempowering their self esteem, leading to vulnerability. Where a lack of equality exists it is important to recognise the need for single gender work. The dynamics of every mixed group is different but again it is important to develop trusting relationships before attempting single gender work in groups or individually. Whilst it may be uncomfortable the behaviour and attitudes of men needs to be challenged. Often this needs effective work from the male worker with the young men and from the female worker with the women. For example, it is important to work with young men, who are often in crisis, to assist them to catch up with the maturity of young women. It also allows time to challenge their learnt sexism and in some areas, their domestic violence.

We must empower young women to also understand that this can be a powerful area of work to bring changes for them, to gain self confidence and gain skills in being more assertive. One of my developmental areas from detached youth work, whilst working with young dads, is that of giving mum's equal support and encouraging them to use the female youth worker/project for support. This in turn makes the mum support the dad's involvement with their children in the dads' group. Again, a holistic approach to working with young people proves to be successful.

So, it is important to look before you leap into working with young women but it is important for male workers to be working with women too. If this does not happen it is discrimination against the young women on your patch.

Chapter 4

Are You up for it?

Relationship Building with Individuals and Groups

As a youth worker we often meet young people at the age of 13-14, spend time in their environment, on the street corner, creating dialogue. Once acceptance has been negotiated into young people's space this can lead to a relationship building phase from 13-16 years, via group work, project work, individual work, residentials and activities. This allows a natural progression for the young person, from the ages of 16-25 years, to work with the detached youth worker, on a voluntary basis. The youth worker can then use these secure, real relationships to use a person-centred holistic approach around issues such as employment, health, housing, parenthood and so on. Dialogue and negotiation will determine the route taken not pre-conceived learning outcomes.

Key elements to consider when working with individuals

Once a real relationship has developed, on a voluntary basis, the individual young person decides whom they trust and who they would like to help them, whether a male or female worker.

Whilst working at South Shields I built up a relationship with an individual young man, via detached youth work. Barry was a very bright, bolshy young man, with a criminal record. Barry had failed with many other professional agencies but developed a real relationship with myself as a detached youth worker. Our relationship began with a number of activities with his mates and over the period of a year developed into an individual relationship. I then encouraged him to apply for a place on the youth development programme with Raleigh International, as I felt he needed a new experience to break away from peer pressure and lifestyle.

Barry was interviewed by Tim Burke, from the *Young People Now* magazine, on his return from a three month Raleigh experience in Guyana. His interview perhaps gives the exact insight into young people's reasons for working with certain people and agencies.

→

'As for many others, employment (for Barry) was not a realistic option and the only Youth Training place on offer would have left him worse off than on benefit. He describes his life then as "get up, get stoned". Criminal convictions followed: Burglary, theft – the normal sort of stuff.'

Despite the going-nowhere lifestyle, Barry was and is no dead-beat. He's clever, passionate and demanding of other people. The professionals appointed to help him sort himself out were generally no use to him: 'Clueless – just in it for the job. But you know straight away when you see one's that's in it for the people and then you can get on with it.'

One of the professionals Barry had forged a good relationship with was the local detached youth worker Mike Burgess. When the South Tyneside Task Force told Mike they could sponsor two people for Raleigh International, Barry's chance to get more experience was there.

Barry's programme was a three-month expedition to Guyana carrying out medical surveys, rebuilding health clinics and completing some environmental projects. His mates were a bit cynical: 'A lot thought I'd never do it, but that just gave me more incentive'.

It did not all go smoothly but, says Barry, he came back a different person, with a different outlook on life entirely.

He highlights three areas that made a big impact on him: the environment, the local people and – despite the unpromising beginning – the relationships forged with some of the other Raleigh venturers.

Meeting and working with the Guyanese led to a big reassessment of his own life. 'They've got nothing. They have no choices, they are right down to the basics of life. When they're very young they have to learn the limits of what they can expect, yet they are really happy at the same time.'

Back in South Shields, this translated to a new determination to follow his own way. Mike Burgess says Barry has become a lot calmer, not so quick to lose his temper. He also points out that Barry is making a conscious effort to separate himself from those peers who have a negative effect on him.

He has started college and is doing courses in psychology, sociology, computing and basic counselling.

→

It's easier when you are in a hole to think, 'Oh, I'm a victim of circumstances, it'll always be like this'.

Barry reflects, 'I looked at myself honestly and I didn't like what I saw. Out there, away from everything I had nothing to do except think about what I wanted. When I went out it was formless but it's a lot clearer in my head now. There's no way I'll just do what my mates expect me to do. At the end of the day I'll do what I want to do'.

His new-found sense of purpose has also enabled him to overcome a drug habit that was getting in the way of his personal development.

'Dope is a way of escape, it's a way of sticking two fingers up to authority. I didn't want to be dominated by a drug. I'll still get stoned sometimes but I can take it or leave it now I've got the motivation to do something else.'

(Burke, 1994)

Barry continued his personal development by attending university and presently is employed as a detached youth worker in Birmingham, now building relationships and motivating young people.

As can be seen from this one example of many successes during my career, this can only be achieved through long-term commitment from the detached youth worker. Real change can only be achieved through long-term funding of detached youth work which is valued and achieves real outcomes for young people.

Long-term commitment was the vital ingredient for success in the following example. Sadly after building a relationship with one young person through detached youth work, he was sent to prison for a section 18 offence. Throughout his sentence I visited him in prison which proved invaluable for continuing to build our relationship. This allowed me to support him when he returned to the community on completion of his sentence. We then went on a roller-coaster ride of highs and lows, from Raleigh and employment, to 'Do you know this man?' being the headline above a picture of a man (the same young person) swinging around in a tree in the Bigmarket in Newcastle, following an FA cup match. He had to hand himself in to the police! Eventually, after five years of long-term commitment from myself he then became a millennium volunteer and gained employment.

Long-term commitment is a necessity for the youth worker to achieve success with individuals but informal education is a two-way street. Never underestimate the amount of knowledge young people can pass on to the detached worker, such as why young people take drugs, their experience of homelessness, knowledge of youth sub-culture and the energy/enthusiasm they have for enjoying life.

When working with individuals there is always a fine line between commitment and involvement. Some issues that young people present are complex and stressful. For this reason it is important not to cross the line from professional conduct to becoming personally involved.

> Whilst working in South Shields a young woman, who we had built up a relationship with via detached youth work, presented herself with a fractured skull due to a dispute with a lodger. Following treatment at the hospital a positive professional social worker, who also worked with the same young woman, became involved. We proposed a woman's refuge but she made the decision to go back to live with the lodger, also asking us to return her there. The social worker clearly stated that she could return if she wanted to but we would not take her. She left and I questioned the social worker as to why he had refused to return her home. He stated that professionally we had done all we could, but we could not be responsible for taking her back into a violent situation. This was a positive learning experience for myself as I realised the importance of not stepping over the boundary of professionalism, to following what emotionally you feel is correct.

Even when detached youth workers are clear of the boundaries between professionalism and personal involvement, it is often very challenging to not be affected by working with young people who are not OK. Working with individuals, as with other aspects of detached youth work, can lead to feelings of isolation, fear and failure. Therefore it is of great value and importance to identify an experienced detached youth worker, outside of your organisation, as a non-managerial supervisor during your reconnaissance period/career.

> In my first job as a detached youth worker I argued successfully to my line manager that my first training need was for them to pay for a non-managerial supervisor. He met me once a month for the first year and bi-monthly after this. If a suitable person is identified it can be a professional support mechanism which will aid your development emotionally and professionally. My non-managerial supervisor, whilst providing emotional support, has assisted me to develop and deliver good quality work in a professional style. Thanks Steve B!

Key elements to consider with groups or project work

As a detached youth worker the importance of spending time talking to young people, playing street games such as pitch and toss, and generally having a laugh must not be under valued. During these informal interactions a whole range of topics, ideas and issues are often discussed. As a walking resource it is often important to promote and educate young people of how to use our (detached worker/walking resource) skills to their benefit, whilst not sounding too eager straight away.

Walking resource

From detached work you can develop in any number of directions. Arranging an activity with some groups, such as to a bowling alley, can be a useful 'getting to know you' activity. Helping an individual, issue based/group work, is what I call project work. Project work is when young people initiate an idea e.g. a graffiti art project, which is clearly working on a piece of young person led youth work and which should come to an end after the completion of the project.

An example of project work I did in South Shields, also involved group work and issue based work around racism and drugs. I first made contact with a lively group – who used to hang about the local park – whilst on a detached work session. As we were walking past a shelter in the park, I heard a rumble? Looking up, I saw a cheeky, smiling lad rolling a small boulder off the roof of the shelter towards myself and my co-worker! Being alert and nimble is often an asset for detached workers!

A few weeks later, on a cold, wet and windy evening, on a detached work session I came upon the boulder rolling group, sheltering from the rain. Sitting huddled together we talked for over an hour about a variety of subjects. One of the group, Lisa, complained of being branded as a troublemaker by adults. She wanted to prove that this was not the case, and came upon the idea of organising a Nelson Mandela street party – with my help. I agreed to offer assistance, but admit to having serious doubts as to whether the young people would follow the idea through, coupled with a hope that it would be a very rewarding experience.

The group involved were young people who were not attracted to other forms of existing youth work provision in the area. So, trying to be flexible, I set about building relationships with the young people as individuals and as a group. Our starting point was to send a letter, to the deputy director of education for the local council, stating the group's aims for organising the event, as written below: →

Dear Sir/Madam,

We have put an idea across to Mike Burgess for help with organising a street party for celebrating the release of Nelson Mandela. We have all thought about this carefully and thought it would be an exciting idea for us to be organising an event for the local public.

We have also thought it would be a good way of keeping teenage children off the streets and help us to do something that they enjoy doing. We are also fed up with being branded as trouble-makers and want to do something positive and prove to adults that we can achieve something meaningful to the local community. We have thought about this carefully and raising money for the famine in Africa is showing you that young people care for what is happening and do not just overlook these positions.

Would you please give us a chance to prove to you that not all of us teenagers are cabbages and trouble-makers. Please give us a chance to achieve something meaningful. We have even thought of involving the disabled group from the John Wright Centre if they are interested in helping us put it across to the public, like making leaflets, and developing ideas for fundraising events.

Yours sincerely,
Lisa Wright (aged 16)

The group decided to meet once a week, with each meeting involving different young people as the number of new contacts increased. Task sheets were used to discuss the organisation of the event. Time was also spent talking about the issues around South Africa, such as racism, apartheid and the Oxfam Frontline Africa Campaign.

After a few months the group developed into a hard core of 11 young people, mostly women. Leading up to the event short, achievable tasks were agreed by the group. These included making a banner and attending the Frontline Africa fundraising launch at the National Garden festival at Gateshead.

The completion of these tasks ensured continued enthusiasm and commitment to the final event. This was borne out by the group's response to their visit to the Garden Festival. They were especially delighted at having been on local television with their banner. The group finally believed that Mandela Day was possible.

The programme was then finalised. The group designed posters advertising the event and motifs for tee-shirts which they sold. They also met the guest speakers and applied for grants.

→

Eventually it was all set. On a fine day in June the Mandela Day did come to South Shields. One individual did ask: 'Is this Mandela bloke coming?' Maybe some day, but not on June 16th. More important, was the fact that this event had been organised by young people for the local community and they completed all of it with perseverance through a long process, gaining valuable skills and self-confidence.

I was rewarded personally by the knowledge that I had helped individuals to develop. The event was the young people's idea, on their terms and at their own pace. It initiated the development of an effective relationship between a detached worker and young people – and proved a point.

(Burgess, 1990)

→

The educational process the young people went through was indeed valuable. Educating the young people to the dangers of solvent abuse and safer practices of using solvents, e.g. spraying onto their sleeves rather than directly into their mouths, was a very positive outcome reducing risks to their health. The African Band, who only played for half an hour, instead of an hour, made the group angry and aware of the need for agreed written contracts, not verbal agreements. The group identified another young person of the same age as them, to talk as a guest speaker, on apartheid in South Africa. This was successful peer education.

The most amusing moment was when a detached work colleague, Morris, with his band, as the support act for the African band, announced he was going to sing the song 'PC99'. The band then started singing 'F*** Off PC99'! Standing next to me was my principal officer, in his suit and tie. Looking horrified he retorted, 'They can't be singing that!' To which my reply was, 'They are!' and laughed.

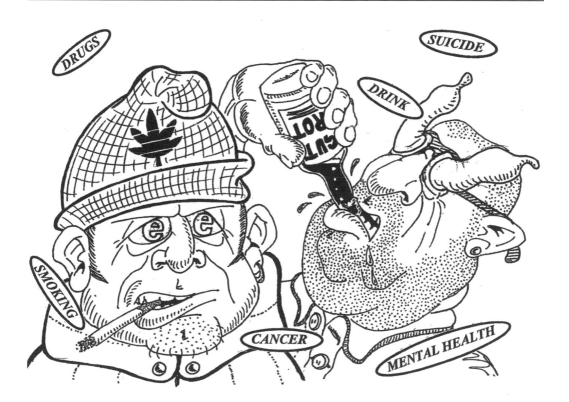

"Are you up for it???"
The characters portrayed above are based on fiction. Any resemblance to
any young people reading this is totally unintentional, honest!

Another example of project work is that of 'Longbenton Lads Health and Fitness Group: Are You up for it', which has been used both in *Changing Places: Young People and Community Action* (Huddleston, 2002) and as part of the Open University course on 'Understanding health and Social Care' (K100).

A group of men, contacted via detached youth work, was set up initially through a common interest in mountain biking. This developed into a lads' health and fitness group, starting in June. Following this they requested help in setting up a young person led group. There was, at that time in Longbenton, a high level of ill health amongst men in general. Mental health problems amongst men are increasing due to both poverty and unemployment.

One of the group's first projects was to arrange a health and fitness awareness day, for young men living on the estate. As stated by the young men, 'Mental health was one area of men's health that the group thought most men in Longbenton suffered at some time in their life, but don't talk about'. Sadly, a good friend of the group committed suicide at the age of 21. This was a difficult time for us all. The group decided to buy a wreath for Craig out of the funds…This is what Micky, one of us, wrote on Craig's wreath – we thought it said a lot:

> *I can't believe that I am writing this mate. It seems as though things like this shouldn't happen, especially to someone like you. We've known each other for years and we've had some really good times. So, I would just like to say, I am always thinking of you mate and I know one day I'll see you again. So just remember there's always things people don't forget, and you're one of them.*

The first step in setting up the group was to arrange some healthy activities that would be fun and help everyone to get to know each other better. Initially we had mountain biking alternating with a group meal on the estate. Five sessions mountain biking, six sessions cooking each other meals, whilst having chats all helped the group to get to know each other. Mike's phrase for it is relationship building.

The lads then started looking at men's health in more detail and began to think about the Health Awareness Day. They asked Jim from the Health Awareness Unit to help them think through what they would need to do.

→

We decided to get training in areas of men's health that we wanted to present on the day, so that we could each run our own stands. Each member of the group would cover a different area. We brainstormed some ideas, then we sorted out different tasks:

- fundraising

- practical arrangements e.g. venue, equipment, buffet, publicity, etc.

- professional help

The lads' training was split into ten sessions over a six month period. Some sessions looked at physical fitness. Others took the lads to the North Tyneside Contour Gym and the local Turkish baths.

Fred Suadwa, a part-time youth worker, helped to lead a session on mental health. Fred and Mike talked about low points in their own lives. Gradually we all talked about how you get low but have nowhere to go with your feelings – 'Heads in the shed', feel like your head wants to explode. Lots of us have taken drugs to escape. One member of the group discussed for the first time how he felt when his Mum died 10 years ago.

Jim Robson ran a session on testicular cancer. None of us had ever thought to examine our balls, very interesting information about cancer and frightening; but we felt more aware after. As a result of this session one of us, who had a lump and had avoided seeing a doctor, successfully went to a rearranged appointment. Men often put their heads in a bucket of sand and ignore it.

Anita, a community dietician, talked about healthy eating issues. We tried out different foods. It gave us ideas for healthy food we could cook for people to taste on the Health Awareness Day.

To find out more about men's health needs on the estate the lads decided to design a questionnaire. The best place for this task was Charlie's Chinese in town. We discussed the content and the questions. We wanted separate questions on each of the health areas we were going to cover on the day, as well as some overall questions about men's health. The best idea we had was to offer a prize for filling it in: fill out the questionnaire and you can enter the prize draw.

→

Some frantic running around led to the day itself. The event was opened by a local soccer superstar, Peter Beardsley. More than a hundred people were there. Issues covered included sexual health, mental health, drugs, health and fitness, smoking, suicide, cancer, cooking on a budget, healthy eating and alcohol.

The day was a huge success. Comments from some of the participants were:
> *Yeah, quite impressed. Opened my eyes to look after myself better.*
> *Lots of men's heads are in bits due to no work. Thought it was just me.*
> *Didn't really want to come but found it interesting. Got my blood pressure checked.*
> *Very good information. Lads easy to chat to about health. Surprised they knew so much.*

Following the success of the day an evaluation report entitled *Are You up for it?* was produced by them. The lads all agreed that they had got a lot out of the project. Not only were they much more knowledgeable about health issues but they had also developed new skills, e.g. planning, organisation, fund-raising, questionnaire design and public speaking. More than anything they felt that they had learnt how to support other men in crisis.

(Longbenton Health and Fitness Group)

As can be clearly seen by these two examples of project work, the value of developing young people's own ideas allows for clear ownership by them of the project. If developed at the young people's own pace, and facilitated correctly by the detached youth worker e.g. listening to their needs, a piece of project work can develop into an innovative and successful project.

For example, the night before the Men's Health Day event I began to panic about very few men turning up. The lads reassured me confidently that at least 70 men would turn up from Longbenton Estate, including locals from The North Star pub! Their ownership of their own project made them keen to succeed and sure of their success. Indeed, to my relief, at least 70 men turned up to learn about health from local men. A much more successful turn out than professionals could hope for! As Jim Robson, the Primary Care Health Co-ordinator stated:

> *Peer education, as this is known, is a tried and tested method of effective delivery in health messages. It rarely happens in a community setting. Health professionals and experts are often brought in to talk or display, often with less impact... The delivery on the Health day would put a lot of health professionals to shame. It was simply an example of good practice.*
>
> *Are You up for it* – evaluation report.

Quite often project work remains inadequately evaluated, possibly because of unclear aims and objectives that are not young person led at the outset of the project. Directly after each session with the young people, group evaluation forms and valuable comments and opinions should be recorded by the youth worker and the group. This can then be used to compile an evaluation report of the project.

The importance of clear aims for any project work allows for effective evaluation on completion, as long as finance has been allocated to produce reports. I feel this should be of high priority because it both completes the piece of project work and promotes good practice, giving clear outcomes for funders and managers.

It is important that an effective evaluation mechanism is employed involving the young people in the evaluation process. The piece of project work has then been done on their terms, at their pace, developing their idea and concluded by the evaluation, thus completing the piece of project work. Ultimately an effective relationship will then have been developed between the detached youth worker and the young people. This will then lead to possible individual work and future projects with the young people, once they are re-contacted on the street, in a detached setting.

So, are you up for it?

Chapter 5

Welcome to Las Vegas, North-East Style

Issue Based Work: Gambling

As informal educators issues affecting young people's lives, which are identified via detached youth work, require a measured and professional approach. In South Shields I developed a multi-faceted response to the problem of young people and gambling on Amusement with Prizes (AWP) machines (fruit machines). As educators, the message is to promote responsible gambling by adults and young people and help individuals in difficulty around machine gambling.

Areas to consider when developing issue based work from detached youth work

- During reconnaissance period identify places of gambling.

Walking out on another detached youth work session, smelling the salty sea and feeling the sea breeze whip around my receding hairline, there was no mistaking the blare of the foghorn at the entrance to the River Tyne. Winter in South Shields was not for the fainthearted but there was always the refuge of the arcades which was a great place to keep warm and therefore a haven for young people.

Putting my two-pence street work expenses into the slot machines (it had been a major achievement convincing the council that £25 a week was needed for chips, fruit machines, pool and burgers!) helped us blend into the surroundings.

After observing the fairgrounds and arcades for three months during our reconnaissance period, a few young people seemed to be individually spending a lot of money in both. With an average of 60 to 70 young people frequenting the fairground over a three month period we concluded that this was mainly a positive experience for most young people. However we identified an issue of overuse of the fruit machine gambling in the arcades by some young people.

→

One young person I worked with was Steve, who was a fruit machine gambler. Steve and I discussed his gambling in an article by Tim Burke in *Young People Now* (1992) entitled *Against the Odds*.

> *Most forms of gambling are restricted by law to people over 18. AWP machines are not. Operators of inland arcades operate a voluntary code of practice banning under 18s, but in seaside towns like South Shields the restrictions are rarely imposed. A lot of youth culture in South Shields is based around the arcades…It's where you go to meet the opposite sex, maybe smoke a joint – it's their area, especially on a Saturday night. In that respect they are a positive environment for young people*, states Mike Burgess.

Steve Moore agrees. He reckons the welcoming and exciting environment had far more to do with him becoming an addict than any financial reasons: 'No-one wants to go down to the youth centre with all its rules and regulations: you go down to the arcade. I'd go to the same machine because I'd get to know it, it became like a friend. It's not the money, it's the buzz of it – the buttons, and bells and tunes'.

The arcade managers are only too willing to develop this relationship. Extremely cheap food and drink are available: Steve says they would even bring him a coffee and sandwich while he was playing.

'I was about 15 and had a job on the market. I'd just been paid and went into an arcade. This was the first time I'd ever played a bandit and I put £1 in and won £15. A week's wages – I couldn't believe it. I thought "imagine that every week!"'

The next day Steve's personal nightmare began…he got a job in the local shipyard earning himself £180 a week. 'I had that much money I didn't know what to do with it. It all started to go on the bandits. They became my whole social life. For me, going down to the arcades was like most people's Friday night – I'd spend ages getting ready, I'd get all dressed up, call a cab to take me into town, give the driver a big tip, and walk into the arcade with £70 in my pocket feeling great.'

But he would spend all that cash and still want to spend more. He started borrowing from his Mum, a friend, and then another friend to pay the first back, and so on.

→

Very soon he became aware that friends really didn't want to see him because they knew it would probably cost them money. The shipyard very soon twigged that his repeated absences were not due to genuine illness and he lost his job.

Now accustomed to being a high roller, the search to beg, steal or borrow the money to feed his habit intensified: 'I started selling everything I had – I even found a £10 tin of paint in a cupboard at home, took it in to town and sold it for a quid, stupid things like that…

Steve's self esteem plummeted with his realisation that he had become a thief, liar and a liability to the people he loved … Attempted suicides, crime, probation and loss of the support of his family spiralled him into depression.

'Like other addicts, gamblers spend time in a dreamworld, only for reality to hit, intrude and hit like a hammer' says Mike Burgess. 'They then suffer withdrawal symptoms, and can become highly sophisticated liars.'

- **Raise awareness of gambling: study, visit and look at the theory and practice of gambling.**

Having identified gambling as an issue affecting the young people in South Shields, the project highlighted the need to explore and develop the issue further. Hence the project joined the UK Forum on Young People and Gambling.

I then went on a week's study visit to Berlin to look at German methods of working with young gamblers. I discovered that working with problem gambling was like working with an invisible addiction. After identifying the problem and talking to others during training, putting theory into practice was a challenging and exciting development.

- **Investigate local initiatives, whilst continuing to build relationships with the young people.**

After gaining initial information and training as a worker in the field, I developed practical strategies and looked at our response in the North East of England towards the issues. No other agencies in my area had developed any practical work with fruit machine gamblers. Often with other issues more experienced agencies allow referrals to take place and this can be an effective solution. You can't be a Jack of all trades!

→

Due to the lack of support mechanisms I was left to develop practical strategies. Therefore after initial contact through letters the first meeting of the North East Forum on Young People and Gambling was held. It became a bi-monthly meeting involving several agencies that were developing the work in the following areas:

- A gambling resource pack for interagencies to use.
- Strategies for workers to develop in helping young people with gambling problems.
- The education of adults and young people on the need to gamble responsibly.

It became a forum for exchanging ideas and practice whilst being an effective support network. Various guest speakers attended meetings such as solicitors and licensing officers, to clarify the law and licensing to our members. It also designed a training pack for local agencies to use in educating young people about the need to gamble responsibly and being aware of the dangers.

An action plan was developed, by myself, with an increase in personal and local knowledge being one of the aims. This involved gaining more knowledge, improving local agency knowledge alongside working with individuals.

Continuing professional development was a necessity in order to assist the young people. I attended a training event in Leicester on working with young problem gamblers.

It became obvious that other agencies also needed to develop their knowledge and I arranged a one day regional training event on young people and gambling at Simonside Community Centre for interagencies: probation, social services, teachers, youth workers etc. The UK Forum ran the day's event and it provided an opportunity for agencies to develop practical strategies further.

- **Develop an action plan on your work with gambling, which should include continued professional development partnerships if available.**

Myself and a student, on placement from Sunderland Polytechnic, produced an information pack on gambling. Throughout the year I continued to develop work with young people suffering from gambling. The project continued to develop practical strategies to assist problem gamblers and to further explore with young people the pro's and con's of gambling. It became clear that this would be a long-term initiative.

- **Develop individual work producing individual action plans using methods appropriate to the young person.**

Most of my work has been on an individual basis firstly developing trusting relationships on the surface, with a view to determining a relevant action plan for the particular individual. It was important to clarify certain areas, if progress was to be made:

- Do they really want to stop?
- Which type of gambler are they?

Involve parents when possible to cross check information and to educate and support them to understand and deal more effectively with the individual concerned.

The message is to promote responsible gambling

Steve, the fruit machine gambler discussed earlier, was referred to me by a probation officer. At first we simply discussed whether or not he wanted to stop. Then we looked at the mental and physical triggers that led him to want to gamble. Eventually, we drafted an action plan, putting structure into his day and developing an alternative interest to replace the buzz from the bandits. For Steve part of the rehabilitation process was athletics. A grant from the Prince's Trust enabled him to get some decent running shoes, subsequently joining a club and winning a road race trophy. He gained part-time work and used my support to analyse his weekly plan. Sessions included discussion about how he spent his money, whether he kept to his training schedule and if he had been tempted to gamble. In addition we worked on his addiction using role-play on a visit to an arcade, videotaping it and analysing it afterwards. This released powerful emotions.

Steve, with my encouragement, produced a set of posters to warn other young people of the addictive power of the bandits. Interestingly, Steve, with his gambling addiction experience wanted a strong message – 'Don't go into arcades!' but I persuaded him to use a 'responsible gambling' message. The posters (see the next page) were very successfully marketed by the UK Forum on Young People and Gambling.

Low key therapy and a lot of personal support helped Steve gain a perspective on his past and hope for the future, though he reckons it will take time to fully recover. 'Sometimes I do go into an arcade, but now I spend £1 and come straight out. That makes me feel good. And I've put too much into getting out of it to fall back now.'

Bandits are like a sandwich. The more you add to them, the greedier you become.

REMEMBER...
Responsible gambling is OK, but don't get too greedy!

REMEMBER
Responsible gambling is OK..

...but don't ruin your life on bandits!!!

Remember-responsible gambling

LOOK BEFORE YOU LEAP

DEBT

Bandits can be addictive!

Remember-responsible gambling

ADDICTION

Don't carry Bad Habits

Remember-responsible gambling

Success is measured using the individual's practical action plan in terms of their debts, the urge to gamble, controlling withdrawal symptoms, leisure interests and rebuilding relationships with immediate family. The action plan is reviewed weekly for practical improvements with support from myself and parents. This pinpoints real progress rather than the impression given by the individual's verbal account, which may be based on a personal dream world. I developed the use of drama to explore an individual's dream world in more depth.

This method achieves success only over a sustained period of time.

- **Evaluation and continued detached work completes a revolving circle of training/knowledge, action plans, partnerships, practice, evaluation, detached youth work, development.**

By having clear aims and action plans, an evaluation of the work can easily be completed. Whilst the normal route is a written report, I opted for an alternative of writing an article for UK Forum on Young People and Gambling, called *Detached Youth Work and Gambling* (Burgess, 1992). This process encouraged me to clearly analyse my practice and how it linked to the theory of issue based work. It also promoted detached youth work. This then led to the article quoted earlier in *Young People Now*.

Continuing professional development and learning from young people must always be part of the revolving circle of issue based work. Social education is a two way process. I spoke, at the first National Conference of the UK Forum on Young People and Gambling, about the positives and negatives of arcades and gambling. Once again, when possible, promote good practice in detached youth work.

As a detached youth worker my increased knowledge allowed me to identify and offer assistance to young people during detached youth work sessions in the arcades whilst doing positive work in the arcades with the majority of other young people.

My detached youth work in the arcades subsequently became more focused and effective. Some indicators of young people with a gambling problem could be:

- An individual playing a machine on their own, and not communicating with other young people, but appearing to be mesmerised by the fruit machine.
- A poor physical appearance.
- Young people complaining about a young person constantly borrowing money and not repaying it.

- Young people outside the arcade can appear to be angry and depressed, on a regular basis.

- Young people barred from the arcades by the owners because they are seen as fruit machine whiz-kids, costing the owners money.

Obviously these could indicate a whole range of other problems but only with experience, further observation and dialogue will you be able to establish whether the young person has a gambling problem.

Chapter 6

Every Individual Has the Right to 30% Unemployment!

Issue Based Work: Employment

Working as a detached youth worker, experiencing both town and estate-based patches, the issue of gaining employment was identified during my reconnaissance periods as a key area of need for young people. South Shields had the highest level of unemployment in the North-East at the time I worked there. Often this is an issue which is not seen as a priority for the worker when leaving college but is one of the most important for young people. It is important for your detached project to develop an action plan or strategy for employment which has clear aims and can be developed as the project develops. (See Appendices 9 and 10 *Employment Strategy* and *The Longbenton Ladder to Success.*)

During detached youth work sessions I have observed young people who are bored and lack identity or direction in life. To replace the absence of this, young people naturally take risks and look for a buzz or excitement that can lead to credibility with their peers. This can encourage some individuals into drug-taking or anti-social behaviour. Without young people realising they then distance themselves from employment via criminal records and escaping into drugs.

If we as detached workers successfully promote employment and offer a service on the street corner, as a walking resource, detached youth work can be an effective starting point. Working towards employment with young people offers them an alternative to boredom and lack of direction.

I became aware of the need to link young people on the street corner to up-to-date job cards from the job centre. After convincing the job centre of the value of the detached project having a set of job cards that were up-to-date, I hoped to contact their missing 10% of prospective clients who they could not identify. With a spring in my step I appeared on the street corner with the up-to-date job cards. Pre-planning proved very effective as I had decided to use 'pitch and toss', the young person's own street game, to introduce the cards. Placing different job cards on the ground I then encouraged them to pitch and toss onto the cards. If a coin landed on the card they had to pick it up and explain what type of job it was.

Pitch and toss the youth worker

The importance of using imaginative and fun ways to promote an issue can be the key to interest on the street corner. Young people can then decide, on their terms and at their pace, when to ask for help, if looking for employment. This approach also highlights, to the young people, that detached workers can help them with employment. Discussion during and after the activity allowed me to individually profile young people's career needs, matching young people with jobs.

Figures below proved the value of this approach. In 1998, 50 young people used the job cards and a total number of 44 young people were worked with in depth around employment. By 1999, 60 young people used the cards and 158 young people were worked with in depth around employment (figures from Longbenton Youth Project's Annual Reports 1998 and 1999 – McGuigan, Burgess and Hunt).

Often a starting point can be irrelevant to the issue, but can develop into a useful arena. One such starting point was when I worked in the fairground.

One group of young people were very keen to visit Holland, to smoke dope! They challenged, 'You'll never take us!' Loving challenges and seeing a chance to link their idea to unemployment I agreed to look at an exchange to Arnhem in Holland. The exchange was to be with unemployed, young Dutch people. As Ofsted commented, 'It is within the detached project that most of the current work with young people at risk has developed.

→

For example, as a result of sensitive and effective work by the detached workers, several young men, all unemployed and in danger of being lured into the local drugs culture, participated in a week long exchange to Holland, to meet and work with young people in similar circumstances' (Ofsted Report *Aspects of Community Education in South Tyneside Education Authority*, Ref. 62/94/DS).

The aims of the exchange, agreed by the group, were to:

- Discuss the differences in vocational training for the unwaged in two European countries.
- Bring young people together from urban backgrounds to explore the differences in cultures and foster good relations between young people in Europe.
- Gain skills in fundraising and basic travel planning as individuals.
- Offer alternative options and confidence in search for work in the wider European community and what that entails.
- Discuss with Dutch hosts a return visit.

This was one of the most challenging experiences of my life! The visit was clearly aimed at helping long-term unemployed (2-8 years) young people look at their options, whilst out of their usual environment. Other young people on the estate questioned my sanity embarking on a journey with the thirteen individual characters who made up the group! So did the other worker who returned home half way through the visit! This was confirmed by various incidents. One of the lighter ones being on the return journey on the ferry when the young people were banned from the disco for using oranges, from the buffet, as a mixer. An enormous mound of oranges on a small table brought down the tone of the establishment! They were evicted for using their initiative!

Following the visit the group cleverly named their evaluation report, *Every Individual Has the Right to 30% Unemployment*.

Positive comments from the young people participating in the exchange were:

Got out of England, met different people.

Excellent time. Good, sound hosts. Loved the motorbikes and the social security talk.

While in Holland I got talking to a man who gave me addresses for work. When I got home I wrote to Grundstadt in Germany and 10 days later I got a reply. I got in contact and I will be going over to work on the 20th December.

I believe that travel proved to be educational and built confidence, which encouraged the group to open their eyes to the wider European community.

It is important to look at innovative ways to develop your project's employment strategy. In Longbenton, due to the estate gaining £70 million, of European funding, for regeneration, the idea to explore employment opportunities for young people in the house-building phase seemed a positive move. Having been a joiner in the past I knew the value of having a trade and was aware of trade shortages.

My clear aim was to promote employment opportunities, with other agencies, for young people. The Detached Project, North Tyneside Training Services, housing associations, private builders, North Tyneside into Work Team and Funding and Support from S.R.B. and Europe were all involved. The title page below symbolises the interagency approach to creating employment for young people:

The success of the construction scheme has not only achieved fantastic outcomes for young people, over a six year period, but has allowed the project to raise a large amount of money, to help fund the project.

The value of this issue based work is discussed by Tim Burke, in an interview with myself published in *Young People Now* (2003) 'How Youth Work Can Build The Future':

> *There is an argument that says youth work values are under attack by Connexions-led requirements to concentrate employment outcomes. Well maybe, but what is inescapable is that connecting young people to the world of work is one of the most powerful things you can do for a disadvantaged young person, and high-quality, well resourced youth work can do it.*
>
> *That is the philosophy that continues to inform the involvement of Longbenton Youth Project in a multi-agency employment project that is transforming the life chances of a number of young people in this disadvantaged area of North Tyneside. LYP is a detached youth work project that has been a feature of life on the estate for the past eight years. From the project's first reconnaissance reports employment was identified as a major issue for young people and has been a developing part of the project's strategy. Senior detached youth worker, Mike Burgess sees it as a key issue because once that is sorted and a person has a bit of money in their pocket, other issues in their lives can become easier to deal with.*
>
> *But the important thing for Mike is that any employment focus of their work is a natural outcome of ongoing detached youth work that has contacted and built relationships of trust with local young people. Indeed the existence of that work is the reason why employment can be a success – his evocative phrase for this is that funders must 'fund the baking of the cake, not just the icing'.*
>
> *…The scheme is a partnership… The youth workers from LYP identify young people who may be interested in the scheme, through their regular detached work… the young people know and trust them and will take advice and guidance from them… They then join with the Into Work team to support and prepare them for an interview for a six month training placement. Selection is carried out by the house builders and NTTS with successful trainees given a range of induction courses in construction before on site training begins… The youth workers also use their skills to deliver training in team building to the trainees, and offer on-going personal support as the training progresses.* →

They are a vital intermediary between the young people, the on-site training supervisor, and the NTTS – generally trouble-shooting and helping to smooth out problems. In many ways they are the glue that holds it all together.

The outcome has been the Longbenton Construction Scheme, a multi-agency project creating traineeships, apprenticeships and ultimately careers in the building trade. Over the last four years some 50 young people have benefited from the scheme, with around 20 young people going on to full-time apprenticeships or employment, one of whom went on to become Apprentice Plumber of the Year.

For Mike Burgess the key to this continuing success is that the project has kept focused on what it is there for – youth work… it concentrates on continuing to deliver detached work to 13-16 year olds. This in turn means the project can progress to offer support in the vital transitions faced when they become 16 to 19 year olds…One of the trainees agrees, 'I'd known Mike since I was 12, we'd done some fundraising for this group we formed and he put me forward for this'.

Standing at the edge of this site in a hard hat with a well-stocked tool belt, the trainees must send a powerful message to other local young people that it is possible to carve out a future…One trainee confirms this 'It's difficult for some young people in Longbenton to see the point in trying to get a job when they can get more on the dole. If there are more people like me around we can help them to see things in the long-term'

There are more winners from the success of the scheme. North Tyneside has looked at the results and is now requiring all builders involved in its project to provide training in this way, while partners Wimpey Homes are using the project reports as examples of good practice which is helping them pick up contracts elsewhere.

'If there's a message for youth workers it is that you don't have to do it all,' adds Mike Burgess. 'As a youth worker you should do what you're good at: support young people, be an advocate, work with partners and organisations and deal with conflict. But when you're working with employment, it is one area where you can look back and say I've really made a difference to this person's life.'

I qualify this further in LYP's annual report when I state, 'To go from seeing a young man standing on a street corner bored, to walking past him confidently putting a roof on, will remain a lasting memory for me'.

Long term investment in detached youth work methods can achieve measurable, achievable results and outcomes. The project's achievements in assisting young people into employment were praised by the Ofsted inspectors, for achieving positive training and real outcomes for the young people in the inter-agency construction scheme. After eight years of hard work, our achievements in 2002 were impressive: 19 young women and 36 young men into employment, and 30 young women and 22 young men into training. Totalling 55 into work and 52 into training, approximately a third of our contacts that year.

Looking for innovative ways to develop an established project's employment strategy is the key to an effective and improving service for young people. Continuing detached youth work alongside other work, from using a bottom up approach, will always be more effective than the top down one of Connexions.

Chapter 7
Cowboys or Indians?
Work with Other Agencies and Partnerships

As detached youth workers spending time, money and resources in building real relationships with young people cannot be underestimated. Primarily this should have been on young people's terms and at their pace. If successful this should have allowed you to build a trusting relationship. This partnership between the young person and detached worker is a voluntary one and this needs to be remembered when working with other agencies.

Many agencies that work with young people work 9am-5pm and adopt a top down approach, on issues such as teenage pregnancy, careers etc. that is driven by adults or government policy. It is important to raise awareness to funders and other agencies of the value of detached youth work as the start of the process. As a profession we need to promote the need to fund detached youth work as the first stage towards achieving long-term outcomes. Regular detached work is often confused with outreach work, and thus has been interpreted incorrectly by other agencies. Detached youth workers often help young people develop their own ideas into young person led projects. Some of the most effective work is developed from the young people/community bottom-up approach. Long-term commitment (five years or more) to young people, via detached youth work, has proven to produce effective outcomes. For example, Longbenton Youth Project assisted 11 young people into work in 1997 by working with other agencies: in 2003 the figure was 44 young people.

As detached youth workers it is important to raise awareness with other agencies of the young people's needs, as identified at street level. One example is the lack of input by health professionals in supporting young dads. Following the highlighting of this to a teenage pregnancy co-ordinator, two young dads were invited to deliver a presentation on engaging with fathers at a National Midwifery Conference. The participants of the conference agreed that the level of service given to dads was unsatisfactory and agreed to highlight the importance of including dads and improving their service to them. An empowering experience for the young dads, it also highlights the need to campaign to relevant agencies for action to be taken on the issues that are important to the young people.

It is important to consider the following before working with other agencies:

- It is necessary to draft clear service level agreements/interagency agreements with other agencies before partnerships begin. This allows you to charge for the detached work already undertaken with the young people or to have a clear statement within the agreement recognising the value of the detached work, the time and cost of resources given to build relationships with the young people.

- The need to assess whether you can effectively work with another professional, in the best interest of the young person, must take priority. For example, certain agencies such as the police, need to be kept at arm's length as their agenda is different to the ethos of detached youth work. It is necessary for the police to control young people whereas our ethos is to empower young people within the rules of the law. Intelligence led detached youth work for the police is not detached youth work as it is social control, not social education or equal opportunities as it targets only disruptive young people. This is strongly debated by Pete Harris in his article on the issue of introducing curriculum led detached youth work. Harris states, 'A utilitarian approach to the development of detached work – targeting 'hot spots' with 'rapid response' teams, the focus on work set up to address anti-social behaviour or community cohesion, and the funding of work through crime reduction streams must be challenged' (Harris, 2005).

- Promote the bottom-up approach as a long-term approach. Detached youth work and relationship building needs to be paid for and valued by other agencies. Charge for the innovative work, for example, boys talk courses for the local high school will subsidise the detached youth work. A key issue to remember is that if you take time to build a positive relationship with a young person it costs money. A good detached youth worker will have worked with a young person holistically e.g. employment, housing, relationships and so on. Effective outcomes are gained because of this holistic approach which may have taken months or years. Do not then undervalue detached youth work by giving away a piece of the whole cake without it being valued by the other agencies accordingly.

- Before you pass a young person on to another agency or worker ensure it is in the young person's interest.

In my experience I have found working with other agencies invaluable and exciting in delivering an effective service to young people. However, beware of the cowboys! You will spot them by their ability to talk a good story whilst providing no service to young people. They are easily identified into two categories. Firstly, the 'willow trees' who sway whichever way the wind is blowing by chasing funding, i.e. a top-down approach. They attempt to fit detached youth work into funding and they rarely listen to young people's needs as they have their own funding led agenda. Secondly, the 'cabbages' who aspire to sit behind desks and talk about other people's work as they do very little work with young people themselves. They rarely listen to young people's needs as they have little direct contact with them.

True Indians are innovative practitioners, who enjoy and care about working with young people. They will be willing to take risks and value detached youth work as a bottom-up approach to developing a multi-agency response to young people's needs. Such open partnerships, showing clearly each agencies payments and defining their roles, will improve the delivery of multi-agency responses to young people's needs.

What are you? A cowboy or an Indian?

Partnerships with funders

Whether funding is from the government or trust funds, good partnerships with funders is vital for without them a project cannot exist. Government funding often uses a top-down approach targeting perceived need in specific areas. Charitable trust funds value preventative work by listening to community needs and will often fund detached youth work as a basis to assist long-term change. The most effective funding is a combination of government and charitable trust funds. Local government commitment encourages match funding from trust funds. This then secures a long-term commitment to the community. In addition it is important for a project to develop income generated work and ideas to show an ability to self-finance.

Developing relationships with funders is as important as developing relationships with young people. Both measure success on the practical action and outcomes achieved. Both require value for money, a cost effective service meeting the needs of the young people and the local community. Both sets of relationships develop mutual trust over time.

Funders require relevant and accurate information on regular timescales. Initially a clear mission statement with aims and objectives for the organisation are required. Additionally a business plan showing budget forecasts, staffing projections and service delivery are vital. In a new project a business plan should be devised after a reconnaissance period has taken place as this will identify areas of need.

Once an organisation is clear of its direction further funding applications can be submitted to funders. Knowledge and experience of detached youth work is an advantage as applications can be tailored to practice at street level. Additionally, funders will assess the skills, qualities and knowledge of the project's trustees and management and will ensure that they are capable of overseeing the finances and management of the project.

Regular communication through reports and visits are required. Positive media coverage of young people would be commendable but unfortunately appears to be rarely achievable! High quality annual reports to promote the work of the project are essential in the present highly competitive environment. Most detached projects have short-term funding which often can mean that staff are inexperienced as job security is poor. Subsequently many projects are short-lived as funding has to be constantly renewed. Therefore, detached youth work requires a professional and business-like approach from both staff and trustees and management. If funders develop an affinity to an area and are shown effective outcomes for their funding then further funding could be possible. However, the need to develop innovative and effective work to meet the needs of a constantly evolving society is both challenging and vital to maintaining long-term funding and long-term results for the young people and their community.

An example of promoting a project jointly to funders and the community is that of Phoenix Detached Youth Project's annual report on interactive CD Rom format. The year's work was brought to life in positive video images of young people taking part in various educational activities. Community involvement is clearly promoted via the inter-generational project allowing young and old to educate and understand each other.

Chapter 8

Leading the Troops out of the Trenches

Managing Detached Youth Work

To manage something as flexible and responsive as detached youth work you clearly need to understand and believe in the method of working. Unless you have experienced detached youth work it is very difficult to manage effectively.

As the manager your most valuable resource is your staff team. Lead your troops not by military dictation but through clear direction and motivation, to go out and offer a walking resource to young people on the streets. Your individual detached youth workers have three main needs that you, as their manager, must respond to. They are physical needs, mental needs and professional needs.

Physical needs

The manager must discuss the following with workers individually:

- For staff to be aware of health and safety whilst doing detached youth work.

- To understand how to observe and understand young people's body language.

- To be safe by not invading personal space and standing in a safe position if the situation is volatile (e.g. side on to a young person).

- To be aware of how risk assessment fits into practice and ensure the detached youth worker is properly equipped with a mobile phone, alarm and is in agreement with other workers as to prompts to leave a situation.

- To ensure staff operate within their comfort zone and don't take risks. Also make it clear how to develop skills by contacting easier groups first.

- Discuss any health or safety issues after the session, review and modify where necessary.

- Certain patches require more street work expenses than others. For example, working in arcades will require more expenses than working on an estate. Flexibility with receipts needs to be exercised as street credibility should come first before asking for a receipt in front of new contacts.

- Ensure that detached workers receive a yearly clothing allowance for a pair of shoes and coat.

Mental needs of individual detached youth worker

Contacting young people on the streets is mentally quite stressful for the individual worker. Therefore it is necessary to have regular line management supervision and ensure that this is discussed then. Discuss how the isolation of the work often weakens their motivation and the direction of the work. Be aware that in the winter months it can often be difficult to keep morale high. It needs to be balanced with positive personal development for individual workers.

Where possible, make available the funds for your detached youth workers to have non-managerial supervision with an experienced detached youth worker independent of your project.

Supervision should explore any groups contacted via detached youth work. Areas such as the level of conflict and dialogue that took place should be discussed. Any issue based needs arising from the dialogue or future ideas or projects should be raised. Each session should highlight their mental health and well being. Also discuss any individuals or groups they are having problems with or are uncomfortable working with. Analyse and discuss ways of overcoming this.

Professional needs

Explore how your staff feel their detached youth work is developing. (Remember to leave the trenches to regularly do detached youth work alongside your staff to review the practice and development at first hand!)

Leading troops out of the trenches

Periodically review staff's detached work evaluation forms and systems, so that accurate information can be obtained and used for outcomes in reports. Promote the value of this and its purpose. Poor evaluation and analysing of dialogue or avoidance of recording detached youth work directly after the session, means that staff are being paid to just walk about!

Celebrate detached youth work success during supervision, however small. This maintains motivation and morale of staff. Be aware that supervision can become problem centred – try to avoid persistent negative discussions.

Ensure individual staff members are aware of the overall picture of how they are funded and what outcomes they have to deliver. Involve staff in future funding plans and business plans.

During supervision discuss how the theory of detached youth work is being linked to practice. Look at any weakness in practice that could be assisted by future training. Review how workers are coping with being quite structured to achieve working in an unstructured environment. Review how workers are challenging, in a supportive manner, the values and attitudes of young people in order to promote equal opportunities, whilst being aware that they are vulnerable on the streets.

Explore the transition from detached youth work into the relationship-building phase, via individual, project, group work or activities. Be aware that they should then return back to detached youth work.

Review any developmental areas of work the youth workers are keen to develop and link to the young people's needs. Out of their detached youth work a good worker should identify issues relevant to their patch, such as domestic violence or gambling etc. This issue then needs to be approached by preparing a clear strategy and action plan. It is essential that the strategy or action plan is evaluated and reviewed through line-management supervision. The key tasks for the coming month, and some measure/outcome of those, needs to be agreed.

Assessing service delivery to young people

If you manage detached youth workers it is important to monitor the number of individuals and groups they work with, alongside the quality of the work. A level two full-time detached youth worker should be involved in initial contact making, relationship building and in-depth group work, as well as being responsible for a developmental area of work for the project. They should, if organised, be able to work with five groups. The worker should be assisted by another member of the team, who they then assist with their groups. It is important to be seen to be treating all groups and individuals equally.

Service delivery depends upon the experience and knowledge of the manager. This appears to be a problem due to short-term funding of detached work which then causes a shortage of experienced detached youth work managers. Detached youth workers are often managed by people who do not understand the work as they are from a different profession or misunderstand the ethos of detached work. Much of the problem has been caused by the lack of long-term commitment to funding detached youth work by local education authorities and agencies which undermine the value and quality of detached youth work to develop and deliver a service to young people. However, there are many well-managed projects that have achieved success against challenging odds. They truly have successfully led their troops out of the trenches! The key to their success is that managing workers in an unstructured environment needs a defined, structured and systematic approach.

Chapter 9

Flying by the Seat of my Pants: A Celebration

Celebrating Detached Youth Work

Following the findings of The Joseph Rowntree Foundation Report of 2004 on reaching socially excluded young people, it is apparent that anyone who follows a career in detached youth work is an extremely rare species! '…street-based youth work appears to be a medium or long-term career choice for very few people'. As I have been described as 'a gob on a stick', love working outdoors and enjoy 'a good crack' then getting paid for this was like a job created in heaven for me! If you genuinely care about young people, like a challenging experience, can be a risk-taker and enjoy being outdoors then this could be the job for you. The great thrill of detached youth work is walking up to young people with butterflies in your stomach to introduce yourself and then two years later to have them return to you and comment, 'Look what I've achieved Mike!'

Some jobs are made to measure for certain people and for me the job fits like a glove. Sixteen years later, with many interesting experiences to relate to, it still remains a challenging and rewarding career choice. Empowering young people to move forwards personally and socially through informal education is still reward enough to continue developing my career in detached youth work.

When entering the profession I looked for material to read (which was a bit of a surprise to those who knew me) on detached youth work and there was very little available and over the years I realised that due to the difficult nature of our job inspiration was needed to guide workers through the difficult periods. I gained immense inspiration and encouragement from my non-managerial supervisor but it would have been beneficial to have some guidelines in writing. Hopefully this book will provide some guidelines or encouragement for those setting out in detached youth work and for those already in the profession to develop good practice. Below are some do's and don'ts which may be useful to you.

Don'ts of detached youth work

- Avoid intelligence led or funding led detached youth work.

- Never work on your own out on the streets.

- Don't be too serious when meeting young people.

- Don't be unstructured in your approach.

- Do not put your agenda first with young people.

- Never forget you are a guest in the young people's environment whilst on the streets.

- Don't stop detached youth work when your project is established.

- Do not fill out detached youth work forms two days after the session.

- Don't avoid issue based work because it is difficult.

- Don't manage detached youth work without any training or knowledge of the area of the work.

- Don't de-motivate staff by your actions as a manager and importantly do not send 'the troops out of the trenches without stepping out yourself'!

- Don't forget you are there to deliver the best possible service to young people in your area.

- Don't forget learning is a life-long experience and even when you are an experienced worker you will not know all the answers.

- Finally never ever be a cowboy, cabbage or willow tree!

Do's of detached youth work

- Do enter the profession because you want to work with young people.

- Do have a sense of humour.

- Do be structured and organised in your approach: 'look before you leap'.

- Always discuss approach methods with your partner before street work sessions.

- Listen effectively to dialogue whilst contacting groups.

- Build relationships with young people on their terms and pace.

- Build a 'bottom-up' approach to ideas and needs, never stop listening to young people.

- Do develop areas of work on issues identified within your patch i.e. the work on gambling in South Shields.

- Do single gender work, talking about your feelings as a male can be difficult but rewarding.

- Do promote good practice.

- Do be aware of how your post is funded and for how long. Argue effectively for long-term funding of at least five years for detached work in order to benefit young people with good outcomes.

- Do look after your physical well being and safety by regularly reviewing practice.

- Look after your mental health by finding a good non-managerial supervisor.

- Do take risks and aim high. Occasionally you may crash and burn but remember you will make a difference to the young people.

- Work hard to improve your youth work delivery and be open to change.

- Do realise youth work can be delivered effectively, even by 'the Bobby Robson of youth work', if you are willing to 'fly by the seat of your pants',

COME FLY WITH ME!

References

Burgess, M. (1990) Proving a Point. *Young People Now*. Issue 19.

Burgess, M. (1991) On the Streets: The Maverick Approach to Youth Work. *Youth Clubs With the Edge*. Issue 62.

Burgess, M. (1992) Detached Youth Work and Gambling. *UK Forum on Young People and Gambling*. Issue 6.

Burgess, M. and Goulding, A. (1999) *Bullet Pointed Guidelines*. National Federation of Detached Youth Workers Conference.

Burke, T. (1992) Against the Odds. *Young People Now*. Issue 44.

Burke, T. (1994) A World of Difference. *Young People Now*. Issue 58.

Burke, T. (1996) New Man, New Masculinity. *Young People Now*. Issue 81 Jan.

Burke, T. (2003) How Youth Work Can Build the Future. *Young People Now*. Issue 165.

Crimmens, D., Factor, F., Jeffs, T., Pitts, J., Pugh, C., Spence, J. and Turner, P. (2004) *Reaching Socially Excluded Young People: A National Study of Street-based Youth Work*. Leicester: Joseph Rowntree Foundation/NYA.

France, A. and Wiles, P. (1996) *The Youth Action Scheme*. London: DfEE.

Goetschius, G. and Tash, J. (1967) *Working with Unattached Youth: Problem, Approach and Method*. London: Routledge.

Harris, P. (2005) Curriculum Debate and Detached Work. *Youth and Policy*. 87, 57-64.

Huddleston, E. (2002) *Changing Places: Young People and Community Action*. National Youth Agency.

Johnson, L., MacDonald, R., Mason, P., Ridley, L. and Webster, C. *Snakes and Ladders: Young People, Transitions and Social Exclusion*. York: Joseph Rowntree Foundation.

Kaufman, S. (2001) Detached Youth Work. In Factor, F., Chauhan, V. and Pitts, J. *The RHP Companion to Working with Young People*. Lyme Regis: Russell House Publishing.

McGuigan, D., Burgess, M. and Hunt, C. (1998) *Annual Report*. Longbenton Youth Project.

McGuigan, D., Burgess, M. and Hunt, C. (1999) *Annual Report*. Longbenton Youth Project.

Ofsted *Aspects of Community Education in South Tyneside Education Authority*. Ref 62/94/DS. Ofsted.

Wild, J. (1982) *Streetmates*. NAYC.

Appendix 1

Sample Job Description

STATEMENT OF PARTICULARS OF EMPLOYMENT

1 POST – DETACHED YOUTH WORKER

2 Your appointment is to the post of Detached Youth Worker with the ....
Youth Project and you are responsible to the .... Youth Project Management
Committee. Your place of work will principally be ....

3 Your appointment is for a fixed term of .... years commencing ....
and terminating on ....

4 GENERAL TERMS AND CONDITIONS

Unless otherwise stated your terms and conditions of employment will be in
accordance with agreements made by the Joint National Council.

5 PAY

Your commencement salary is JNC level .... Scale .... You will be paid on a
.... basis. Where applicable increments will be paid as from the 1st of April
each year.

6 WORKING HOURS

Your normal working week is one of .... hours, however the post will require a
certain amount of work on evenings and some weekend work. The precise details of
your hours of work will be determined by arrangement between you and the
Management Committee. Time off in lieu will be granted by your line manager.

7 SPECIAL CONDITIONS

You may need to travel in order to undertake some of your duties, in such cases
public transport expenses will be reimbursed or an allowance ....p per mile if using
your own vehicle. (The mileage allowance may be reviewed from time-to-time as
appropriate.)

A yearly allowance for the necessary clothing and footwear is available subject to the Management Committee approval.

8 LEAVE ENTITLEMENT

The basic annual leave entitlement for a full year is .... working days which may be taken by agreement with the Management Committee,

You will be required to give .... weeks notice of your intention to take leave. In addition you will be entitled to statutory bank holidays as they occur. The annual leave year shall be from the 1st of April to 31st of March.

9 SICKNESS

i) You are entitled to the first three months full paid sickness leave which reverts to statutory sick pay allowances for any time over and above that period.

ii) If you are absent due to sickness you should notify your line manager on the first day of absence and should sickness continue after the 8th calendar day a doctor's medical certificate should be submitted.

10 MATERNITY LEAVE

The national agreement referred to in paragraph (4) provides for employees to take maternity leave, some of which will be with pay, and to receive other benefits, subject to certain conditions. If employees who have taken maternity leave do not return to work for at least 3 months, they will normally be required to return a portion of their maternity pay. Full details available in JNC handbook.

11 PATERNITY LEAVE

Two working weeks (10 working days) leave will be granted, where appropriate on full pay. This is to be taken within 3 months of the birth of the child.

12 NOTICE PROVISION

The period of notice required to be given by either party shall be two calendar months.

13 **GRIEVANCE PROCEDURES**

If you have any grievance about any matter concerning your employment you should raise the matter with your immediate supervisor. If you wish to pursue your grievance beyond this stage you may raise the matter with the Management Committee. There is no level beyond the Management Committee as a final stage.

14 **DISCIPLINARY PROCEDURE**

The disciplinary procedure is designed to ensure that disciplinary matters are dealt with thoroughly, promptly and equitably.

Outlined in JNC Handbook.

At every stage of the disciplinary procedure you shall have the right to be accompanied by your trade union or other chosen representative to assist you in explaining your actions. You will be informed of this right before every disciplinary interview.

Before invoking the final procedure your management/supervisor should make every attempt to resolve disciplinary matters on an informal basis by discussing the situation with you to avoid the necessity of formal warnings.

The formal disciplinary procedure is described in stages of increasing seriousness to avoid ambiguity about your position. It must be noted, however, that some misconduct is so serious that it will immediately need to be considered under stages 2 or 3.

You will be notified of the level at which any disciplinary action is being considered.

15 **HEALTH AND SAFETY AT WORK**

The .... Youth Project's general policy is that you must have regard to your own safety and that of others with whom you work and to report any concerns immediately to your supervisor or a member of the Management Committee.

16 **PENSION SCHEME**

You have the right to join either a private pension plan or the State Earnings Related Scheme (SERPS). You will automatically be entered into SERPS and your National Insurance Contributions deducted as appropriate unless you notify the .... Youth Project that you have joined a private pension plan.

17 **COLLECTIVE BARGAINING**

You have the right to be in membership of a trade union who can represent you on the appropriate negotiating body and you are encouraged to be so.

Signed .... Date ....

Signed .... Date ....

Appendix 2
Sample Detached Youth Work Guidelines

Detached Youth Work

Detached work is a style of youth work in which the youth worker goes out to meet young people on their own ground – in pubs, cafes, arcades, parks and street corners.

Detached work is an important part of a comprehensive youth work strategy, and should not be seen as a 'knee jerk' response to political or social pressure, be it concern about crime figures, drugs or other disturbances. It is complementary to other approaches, including centre-based provision, project work and outreach work, and a method of social education to young people who may not otherwise have access to youth services. Some young people may have no alternative provision in their neighbourhood; others simply do not wish or feel able to attend the centre, which is there.

The underlying principles and philosophy of detached youth work are to accept young people as they are. Young people who gather on street corners are often viewed as a threat to the community or at risk to themselves. Detached work does not label or judge in this way, workers do not condemn young people because of their behaviour, but they do not condone it either, and will constructively challenge young people about their behaviour, attitudes and perception of self and others.

The basis of the relationship between worker and young people is mutual acceptance and parity – a negotiated relationship in which traditional notions of adult power and authority play no part.

Aims of Detached Work

1. To make contact and be available to young people in the settings of their choosing.
2. To work with young people through programmes of personal and social education, which help them gain knowledge and recognise new opportunities in the world around them.
3. To build effective and meaningful relationships with young people through regular contact, mutual trust, respect and understanding.
4. To identify and respond to the needs and agendas of individuals and groups of young people by developing appropriate strategies for action which are both educational and fun.

5. To support and challenge young peoples' attitudes and actions towards issues such as: unemployment, drugs, alcohol, poverty, racism, sexism, disability, housing, health, sexuality, criminality, peer, parental and community pressure.
6. To enable young people to take more control over their lives and create experiences with them which enable them to make informed choices.
7. To support appropriate action that young people take resulting from their own ideas and suggestions.
8. To work within the framework of equal opportunities.
9. To bridge the gaps in understanding between the local community and young people.
10. To highlight issues affecting young people and act as advocates for and with them within the wider community and world.

Practice Policy Guidelines

For detached work to function effectively, and to ensure that the workers, who undertake the work are adequately supported, each project must develop policy and guidelines pertinent to its purpose.

The responsibility for the development of policies and guidelines lies with the workers and managers of the projects, and these must be realistic, achievable and practical, and set within the context of the available resources and the priorities of the DYP Development Plan.

Detached youth work is not a cheap option, and careful consideration needs to be given to the appropriate resourcing of the work in order to ensure the effectiveness of services to young people, and to protect the values of the work itself, which can be adversely affected by unrealistic expectations and inadequate direction and support.

To assist in this process, the following guidelines may be used as a basis for the development of the project.

Guideline and policies do not exist within a vacuum, and linkage must be made with existing documents. All these should be accessible to workers and managers and be located in a central file within the office base.

1. Training

Youth workers new to detached youth work should receive initial training, which will include a comprehensive briefing about the objectives of DYP, the importance of adequate reconnaissance and methods of contacting young people safely.

There should also be access to information or training related to the legal system, young people's rights, and drug and health related issues.

The management committee will also need some training to ensure that they are able to play a full and effective part in the development of the project, and the support and direction of the workers.

Contact should be made with existing projects, and recognition be given to the importance of networking and mutual support, with particular reference being made to any local, regional or national detached youth work forums and conferences.

2. Supervision and Support

Detached youth work is a method of work that requires strict self-discipline and purpose. This cannot be emphasised enough. There are no opening times or constraints as can be found within building based work, and therefore it is essential that workers are highly motivated, confident and committed to the purpose of developing positive relationships with young people in the settings of their choosing. The major resource is that of the workers, with their particular skills, experience, and knowledge, and the work is reliant upon their abilities and effective practice.

In order to ensure the project maintains purpose and quality, workers should be regularly supervised in accordance with the development policy. The management committee should meet on a regular basis with the workers' reports being the central item for discussion.

Workers should be encouraged to participate in non-managerial supervision, a form of support outside the context of line management and work supervision. Approximately 1.5 hours a month should be made available for this, and where possible a budget allowance made for this purpose.

3. Safety Policy
* *Agreed Working Hours*
  To ensure safety, detached youth workers will be deemed 'on duty' at agreed times and days of the week, and have telephone access to nominated persons from within the management structure. All work should start and finish at an agreed time or site.

  The above does not preclude workers being professional in their judgements concerning young peoples' needs and allowing for flexibility in working arrangements. The nature of the work is not that associated with a strict timetable, as there are times when young people require contact support outside the 'norm' of patterned work. Workers should be relied upon to make autonomous, professional decisions which do not increase risks to themselves or the young people being worked with, but allow for spontaneity and flexibility in addressing certain circumstances.

- *Co-worker*
Single worker posts create unnecessary stress and isolation for the worker, and good practice would dictate that workers work in pairs. This provides mutual support for workers, but can also ensure that there is corroboration of evidence or a witness in the event of accusations from young people or the police. Due consideration should be paid to gender balance in working pairs, and when undertaking the work, workers need to be careful not to put themselves in situations which may leave them open to allegations of misconduct or abuse.

- *Individual Work*
If it is not possible to work in pairs, professional judgement must be used within the context of one's own experience and knowledge concerning safe working practices. Use common sense and apply it. The most appropriate individual work will be that where services are being provided for young people, e.g. court attendance, previously agreed meetings, workshops or groupwork in known venues/settings.

- *Identification*
Workers should carry ID cards with a photograph and name of the workers whilst working. The cards do not guarantee protection, but can assist in establishing a workers identity and legitimate purpose. Loss of cards should be reported both to the management and to police, to reduce the risk of people impersonating workers.

- *Confidentiality*
At no time should the home address and telephone number of the worker be divulged. This information should be kept entirely confidential.

- *Telephone Access*
Workers can carry items which they feel appropriate for safety purposes, e.g. personal alarm, first aid, mobile phone. In some cases the provision of a mobile phone may be necessary, if it is judged that the location of the work is quite 'isolated', e.g. cemeteries or particular circumstances have arisen that have made the area volatile or unsafe. When transport is used for young people, e.g. a minibus for trips and residentials, it is advisable to have a mobile phone as part of the bus's equipment.

- *Working Practice and Legislation*

  Workers are not expected to take greater risks than they would in their private lives, but it is acknowledged that the work will always carry an element of risk to it.

  Workers should meet regularly for mutual support, sharing experiences, information and ideas to aid the development of good and safe practices. Meetings should be nominated and training needs identified from them.

  Workers must work within the law and within other DYP guidelines.

4. Record Keeping

Recordings are an essential and vital reference with regards to contacts made as well as for supervision, monitoring of the work, evaluation and forward planning.

Workers should record their work as soon as possible after sessions worked with young people, and these should be agreed as part of the timed working session.

Records should be confidential to the project.

A simple recording sheet will be devised, and every worker, full, part-time or volunteer will be responsible for completing them on a regular basis. This is an essential element of detached youth work discipline.

5. Evaluation of the Work

The responsive, flexible nature of the work can increase the risk of a project or workers losing focus and direction. It is impossible for detached workers or projects to answer every need and demand of the young people or the community where they live or utilise.

The project must set out its intentions with clear aims, objectives, geographical location and boundaries, and the work must be effectively planned.

Evaluation should be a continuing process, using workers' recordings and findings. Each piece of more formal structured work that might arise should be evaluated alongside and with the young people involved.

6. Confidentiality

Workers need to be explicit with young people and others regarding the boundaries within which they work.

Regarding what a worker is told, the boundary will normally exclude information that is withheld and may leave someone exposed to danger. (DYP Child Protection Policy.)

Regarding what a worker witnesses, the worker may be obliged to contact the police (e.g. serious assault), whilst other situations would require the worker to answer truthfully if later questioned by the police (e.g. smashed window). In either case the worker will not lie on behalf of young people and it is vital that young people know this.

Workers need to be aware that young people may assume through implication that confidentiality goes further than it actually does. The only exception to this is when someone is in such extreme danger that their safety becomes the overriding factor.

Workers would also recognise that it may be expedient for them to make a 'tactical withdrawal', so that they do not witness an anticipated incident. It is ok to say to young people 'if you're going to do that, I do not want to work with you/cannot work with you at this moment in time.'

Managers should appreciate that the worker will sometimes only convey such basic information about a contact as to render themselves accountable. If it becomes necessary or appropriate for the worker to go into more detail than this then the anonymity of individuals should be preserved. Managers should in turn, observe confidentiality, allowing workers to be frank with young people about what they report and to whom, notwithstanding the legal requirements outlined in previous paragraphs.

It is essential to respect the confidentiality of workers' written reports, as the work centres on individuals and groups of young people. Young people should not be identified by this process, or any information used outside the context of the project.

7. Liaison with Other Agencies

The workers and management committee should ensure that the local community, inclusive of other agencies is aware of the presence of the project prior to the commencement of direct work with young people. It is necessary to draw up plans and prepare for the work, by being clear about the area of operation, purpose and intention of the work, and to circulate this information within the local community. Personal contact is the most important in terms of getting to know an area, and the people, and this must be a priority at the onset of any project, e.g. reconnaissance period.

8. Base/Resources

All workers need a reference point, a place where they can attend to administrative and recording needs. An office base needs to be established, with the basic requirements being desk, chair, filing cabinet, telephone, notice board, pens, paper and shelving.

Workers should have access to clerical administrative assistance, so that reports and letters can be produced in a professional manner. The base itself does not have to be in the geographical location of the project, but it should be easily accessible to workers, and in close proximity to the working area. The base must be identified and basic furniture and equipment set up prior to workers being appointed to the posts.

Other elements of resource would include a budget for equipment and repairs, programme, postage, printing and stationery, travel and motor costs, training, supervision (non-managerial), telephone, and streetwork expenses. These would be designated as controllable overheads, but in addition non-controllable overheads would include administrative charges e.g. clerical support, insurance and rent and rates. These are all essential in order to achieve the effectiveness of the work, and the proper support for the workers.

As previously stated, there are other relevant guidelines produced by DYP which impact upon and inform practice, as well as helpful literature from individual detached youth work projects or authorities. It is important that this previous work and experience is acknowledged, as it can assist with the development and planning of the work, and prevent malpractice or mistakes in the setting up of new work. However, it is essential that each project has its own aims, objectives and practice guidelines and that people go through the process of thinking about and establishing procedures for themselves and their own particular set of circumstances. Young people must be provided with effective support, resources and direction.

DEFINITIONS

The terms 'detached', 'outreach' and 'project based youth work' as descriptions of types of work are often confused, and this can lead to misunderstandings about their purpose, and in some instances workers being given inappropriate job titles for the work they are engaged in.

Definitions by their very nature can be a matter of argument and debate, but these following definitions may enable more clarity to emerge concerning the emphases of the work.

Detached Youth Work

Detached work is a style of work in which the youth worker goes out to meet young people on their own ground in pubs, cafes, arcades, parks and street corners. The basis of the work is in accepting young people as they are, not because they have been labelled or described as 'disadvantaged', 'delinquent' or 'truant'. Workers do not have to manage or be responsible for a building, allowing them to be more flexible, responsive and responsible to the young people they meet.

Outreach Work

Outreach work involves contacting young people outside a centre. It is an extension of work linked to a base, such as a youth centre or project, and can be used to encourage young people to make use of existing provision. It aims to reach young people in the name of the centre or project, and in some circumstances it will bring young people back to the base, developing work with them there.

Street Project Work

Street project work has a specific targeted objective, whether that be a particular type or grouping of young people, or a definitive purpose linked to measurable outcomes. This could mean for example working specifically with young people who have been identified as 'drug users' with the aim of reducing harm to themselves and the wider community, or working in a particular locality with the objective of reducing criminality amongst young people.

Produced by Liverpool Youth Service – Detached Youth Work Guidelines.

Appendix 3

Induction Pack

INDUCTION PROGRAMME FOR NEW EMPLOYEES/STUDENTS

Date completed

BACKGROUND TO .... D.Y.P.
History of the project/area covered (patch)   _____
Reconnaissance period   _____
Aims and objectives   _____
Developmental areas of work   _____
Funding of the project   _____

PHOENIX BUSINESS PLAN   _____

PHOENIX FUNDING STRATEGY   _____

GUIDELINES/POLICIES OF THE PROJECT
Detached youth work guidelines   _____
Child protection   _____
Equal opportunities   _____
Health and safety   _____
Sexual health guidelines   _____
Liability insurance   _____
Risk assessment policy   _____

RISK ASSESSMENT TRAINING
Detached youth work   _____
Individual work (gender)   _____
Group work   _____
Activities   _____
Outdoor education   _____
– Kayaking   _____
– Karting   _____
– Mountain biking   _____
Hazardous activities form   _____
Minibus transport   _____
Accident book and procedures   _____
Parental consent forms   _____

Date completed

STAFFING/VOLUNTEERS

Payment of wages

Staffing structure

Appraisal system

Line management form

Identify non-managerial supervisor

Line manager in absence

I.D. card

Personal alarm

Clothing allowance

Grievance procedure JNC

Sickness roles responsibility

Holiday entitlement forms

Claiming travel expenses

Keys/office/procedure

Petty cash and procedures

Time sheets/weekly

COMMUNICATION

Effective use of a diary

Use of fax

Use answer machine

Guidelines and use computers

Internet guidelines

Effective use of meetings/time

JOB DESCRIPTION/CONTRACT

Clear understanding of roles/responsibilities with line manager

Training needs personal/project

Developmental areas of work

In full-time learning .... agree to a balanced approach

to assist learning to benefit both parties

Staff to look at how they fit into the team

Aware of all other staffs' roles and responsibilities and

developmental areas

Knowledge of other agencies and partnerships

Role of company trustees

Agree relevant agency visits with manager

Date completed

ADMINISTRATION

Detached youth work evaluation forms/risk assessment

Group work forms issue-based/activities

Annual report/report writing

Promotion of work funders/management/media

Filing systems

Consent forms parents/insurance

Risk assessments/policies into practice

Minibus access/procedures QVLYP

Computing/e-mail systems

Ordering resources

PROJECT RESOURCES

Peer educators DJ mixing

Storage of kayaks and procedures

Assess to LYP bikes/go-karts

Towing with a minibus

YOUTH WORK PRACTICE

Sources of funding for groups

Detached youth work practice review

Evaluating and recording

Report writing

Dealing with conflict and procedures

Developmental work action plan

Time-management university/work/placement

NAME .... has completed ....

D.Y.P. staff induction on .... (date)

SIGNED .... (Line manager)

Appendix 4

Probationary Non-managerial Agreement

NON-MANAGERIAL SUPERVISION

Name _____

Work address _____

Contact numbers home _____

                          work _____

                          mobile _____

Breakdown of monthly sessions in initial year of non-managerial supervision

Session 1   First year as a detached worker: reconnaissance and beyond.

Session 2   Training needs.

Session 3   Evaluation of first three months supervision.

Session 4   Evaluation/recording of detached youth work.

Session 5   Improving weaknesses and developing strengths.

Session 6   Developing skills in group work, project work and individual work.

Session 7   Effective management of time and resources.

Session 8   Looking after your mental and physical health.

Session 9   Evaluation of initial year and discussion of needs for further non-managerial supervision.

Non-managerial supervisor _____

Detached youth worker _____

Appendix 5
Federation for Detached Youth Work

THE FEDERATION FOR DETACHED YOUTH WORK
Federation for Detached Youth Work, POB 35124, London SE5 9XA.
Tel: 07789 396200; enquiries@detachedyouthwork.info; www.detachedyouthwork.info

The Federation for Detached Youth Work (FFDYW) was formally launched in 1996 where it gained charitable status. It is an organisation for detached youth workers, inspired by their practice needs and constructed by their desire to inform, organise and improve the practice of detached youth work nationally. It is essentially a 'grassroots' organisation; being established solely through the voluntary efforts of detached youth work practitioners across the country. It did not come about overnight, but was the product of initial deliberations conducted after a national conference held at Sheffield during 1992 and philosophically, dates back to the Keele conferences of the 1970s and 1980s.

MISSION STATEMENT
'The Federation for detached youth work exists to support, promote and develop detached youth work. This will be based on the active participation of detached youth workers to ensure their needs are met through effective communication, advocacy, training, advice and information.'

BENEFITS OF AFFILIATION
*   Resource library specifically in detached youth work (DYW)
*   Statements on social policies affecting DYW
*   Access to our national database of workers in specialised fields of DYW
*   National and localised needs-led training
*   Newsletter providing the most recent information on the development of DYW nationally
*   Access to the most recent social polices and The Federation's perspective
*   Regional forums offering localised networking, support and training
*   Careers opportunities
*   Access to professional advice and information regarding all aspects of DYW national representation and advocacy for all DYW
*   Access to and use of national guidelines in DYW
*   Free professionnal legal advice from two solicitors in education and crime

Appendix 6

Sample Recording and Evaluation Form

DETACHED YOUTH WORK RECORDING AND EVALUATION FORM

Recording

Date and time: Workers:

Aims and objectives:

Place of contact	Known males		Known females		New males		New females	
	14-18	19-25	14-18	19-25	14-18	19-25	14-18	19-25

Level of contact: (observational, verbal communication, level of dialogue)

Overall impression:

Issues raised or experienced:

Outcomes and future action:

Appendix 7

Sample Recording and Evaluation Form for an Interagency Visit

AGENCY INFORMATION

Name of worker: _____

Name of agency: _____

Type of agency: formal/informal – (please circle)

Address of agency: _____

_____ Postcode: _____

Telephone number: _____ Mobile: _____

What does your service offer to young people? _____
_____

Background of agency: _____
_____

Background of the worker: qualified/unqualified – (please circle) _____
_____

What do they think are the issues affecting young people in this area? _____
_____

Are there any other agencies in the area that we may not be aware of? _____
_____

Collection of leaflets about the agency: Yes/No (please circle) _____
_____

Do we have a future working link with the agency? _____
_____

Attitude of worker? _____
_____

Appendix 8

Risk Assessment Policy

Insurance Liability insurance cover for staff renewed March each year to cover detached youth work.	**Action** Manager is responsible for renewing each year. Staff aware of liability insurance cover (in case of accident do not accept responsibility).
Guidelines Clear understanding of detached youth work guidelines for .... Detached Youth Project.	**Action** Staff to read and understand.
ID card Each member of staff is responsible for obtaining, and getting signed by trustee.	**Action** Staff to carry ID card on all detached youth work sessions and responsible for replacing at own cost if lost.
Safety equipment Each pair of workers must carry the project's mobile phone.	**Action** Carry at all times, especially on detached youth work sessions, for emergencies and safety.
Staffing levels Two members of staff to do detached youth work sessions.	**Action** No member of staff is to work individually on detached youth work sessions.
Weather and daylight Assess risks weather can cause.	**Action** Change of plans may be needed on some nights e.g. bonfire night, snow etc. Assess the risks of working dark nights.
Preparation for detached work Aims and targets discussed for each session. Gain knowledge of area or escape routes. Observational period.	**Action** Workers agree on action prior to session. Know way around area and discuss escape routes. Don't take unnecessary risks e.g. with a group at the bottom of a cul-de-sac. Identify easier groups to approach first if new in post. Identify where groups hang out. →

Contact making	Action
Agree on target group.	Discuss if both confident, who talks first and how to support colleague.
Observing staff safety and level of risk.	Agree on clear signal when risk identified and need to leave situation, agree safety route.
Awareness of when young people are at risk e.g. hanging out in a dangerous building.	Staff need to explain the risks to the young people and encourage leaving. Contact the owners of the building to secure the site.
Physical safety **Action**	
Assess area young people approached are in.	Safe for staff.
Safe distance to stand.	Stand at arm's length and stand side on when meeting new groups.
Observe young people's body language.	If young people turn away when they see you etc. it is not the time to approach.
Young people using drugs.	Staff assess the risk, don't stay around if young people are taking drugs.
Accusations by general public, police, young people etc. **Action**	
Witness injury or accident whilst on detached youth work session.	If qualified, assess danger, administer first aid, dial 999.
	Assess if person at risk, staff stay together to support each other and record accident/ injury.
Accusations.	Don't admit liability, always stay with co-worker, don't be alone with young people.
Evaluation **Action**	
Any incident of any kind must be reported to line manager directly after the session or at the venue if urgent.	Seek advice, manager record incident from both workers. Fill in accident book as soon as possible at office base if injury sustained. DO NOT ACCEPT LIABILITY. Contact insurers via line manager.

Appendix 9

Employment Strategy

THE OUTCOMES FOR YOUNG PEOPLE

Over the past year our employment strategy has clearly been developing, with a good link with other agencies increasing to allow a better service to young people. The project has worked with forty-four young people in depth, fourteen young people have gained full-time employment eight young men, and six young women. Eleven young people have gained training opportunities, ten young men and one woman.

Outreach Careers Service
14 Young people into employment

Job Cards from West
Moor Job Centre
50 young people

Training Opportunities
11 young people
(6 Nomad)

**LYP
Employment Strategy**

43 young people
Individual Employment
Skills

4 young people into
voluntary work

Setting Up Own Business
4 young people
supported

Personal Development
1 young person – Tall Ships Race
and Farrimer Trust

Appendix 10

The Longbenton Ladder to Success

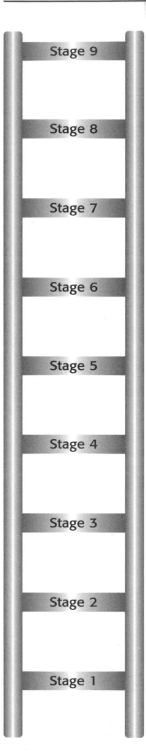

Stage 9 – Full Time Employment
41 young people into employment, 20 from job cards.

Stage 8 – Into Work Team
Developed effective working practice with Into Work matching people to jobs.

Stage 7 – Training Opportunities
33 young people training opportunities, 10 through the local construction schemes.

Stage 6 – Setting Up Own Business
1 young person supported to set up their own business.

Stage 5 – Personal Development Courses
2 young people (Personal Development Course), 2 Raleigh International.

Stage 4 – Voluntary Work
Voluntary work, 5 involved in voluntary work, 2 Millennium volunteers, 2 LYP Team Builders, 1 Go-Ken Project.

Stage 3 – School Careers Development Work
Linking Science and Maths to Curriculum Training. Pack given to both Secondary Schools, Cardboard Houses given to three primary schools for training via Wimpey Homes. Recruited young people from both schools onto construction scheme.

Stage 2 – Careers Outreach
Careers outreach, 26 young people involved with job search, support with applications, C.V.s or referred to the Into Work Team.

Stage 1 – Job Cards
98 young people look and discuss job cards during detached youth work.